In praise of Bill Somerville
and Philanthropic Ventures Foundation

"Every day Bill Somerville demonstrates that a foundation can be instantly responsive, sensitive, interested in your ideas and helping as many people as possible."

—Ed Nathan, Vice President, van Löben Sels/Rembe Rock
Foundation, former Executive Director, Zellerbach Family Fund

"Bill is my hero—a friend to all of us who care about our communities, our children, our country; someone who can see the great ideas when others just see chaos or problems; someone who listens and reaches down to the grass roots to discover new trends, new ideas."

—Catherine Milton, Founder, Friends of the Children,
former Executive Director, Save the Children

"Working with Bill Somerville continues to be a joy in every regard. It is difficult to imagine how we could accomplish much of our grant-making, both regionally and internationally, without his assistance."

—Thomas C. Layton, President,
Wallace Alexander Gerbode Foundation

"Bill Somerville has inspired my community work in ingenious and provocative ways."

—Alice Waters, Founder and Director, Chez Panisse Foundation

"Bill Somerville has the right idea about philanthropy. Respond quickly and responsibly. Pick the causes that help people at the core."

—Phyllis Koshland Friedman, President,
Friedman Family Foundation

"Bill Somerville has taken philanthropy from the traditional grant-making paper shuffle to the neighborhoods and classrooms. His creative and entrepreneurial spirit, coupled with his willingness to experiment and trust, has reinvigorated crucially important nonprofit groups while helping to save lives on the edges of American society."

—Jackie Speier, former California State Senator

"Bill Somerville tells the truth, even to those who don't want to hear it. He represents hope and practicality. He's been a personal inspiration to me and countless others."

—Jan Masaoka, former Executive Director, CompassPoint

"Bill Somerville has helped us deliver resources to the heroes of the human rights movement in countries around the world."

—Regan E. Ralph, Executive Director,
Fund for Global Human Rights

"Had it not been for Bill Somerville, my career in philanthropy might never have gotten off the ground. His mentorship and his legacy gave me the guidance and platform to keep learning and serving. I am forever in his debt."

—Sterling K. Speirn, Executive Director of
W. K. Kellogg Foundation, former Executive Director,
Peninsula Community Foundation

"When I wanted to set up a fund to aid disadvantaged children in memory of my late wife, I naturally thought of Bill Somerville and PVF. I have been grateful for the way the funds are being utilized—much more creatively and effectively than I could have done on my own."

—Marty Tarshes, longtime PVF Donor

"Bill's style of leadership provides Stanford students with new perspectives on public service. Bill is inspiring a new generation of young people to strengthen their commitment to creative and constructive social change."

—Kent Koth, Service Learning Program Director,
Haas Center for Public Service, Stanford University

"PVF assembled a meticulous account of their work with public school music programs, including testimonials and photographs from the teachers. I rarely encounter such care in presenting the results of grants—nor do I commonly see such gratifying poignancy in their effects."

—B. Stephen Toben, President, Flora Family Foundation

"Bill Somerville's no-bureaucracy, want-to, can-do, will-do attitude and creativity in assisting unique giving make the difference."
— Duncan Beardsley, Director, Generosity in Action

"PVF is a rare, wonderful asset in the Bay Area giving community. Our foundation can only hope to strive for such efficiency and successful risk-taking. Bill Somerville has set the bar very high indeed."
— Julie Shafer, Executive Director, Silver Giving Foundation

"Bill Somerville has helped our donors, staff, and board understand what a community foundation, at its best, can achieve. All of us have gathered inspiration for the mission ahead."
— Sue Brown, President, Sioux Falls Area Community Foundation

"Bill Somerville continues to be a creative genius, the epitome of true charity, and an irreplaceable source of loving guidance and innovation."
— Patricia Bresee, Board Member, Silicon Valley
Community Foundation, prior Commissioner,
Superior Court of San Mateo County

"Bill lets the creative juices flow, always saying 'Let's do it' and never 'We can't'…He has helped us immensely over the years."
— Adele Corvin, President, Morris Stulsaft Foundation

"The Scottish Community Foundation has never been the same since Bill Somerville came to help us. We are bigger and better, yet quicker on our feet, and we have many, many donors."
— Alan Hobbett, former Executive Director,
The Scottish Community Foundation

"I admire your work at PVF tremendously for advancing the practice of philanthropy, and making it more transparent for the community."
— Carol Lamont, Program Officer, Community Development,
The San Francisco Foundation.

"Bill Somerville is an energetic and tireless 'servant' of our field. Many, many years ago, Bill came to Indiana for a session with staff and board of about four community foundations. Many of his suggestions were taken at that time and have become truly our culture of access and no red tape!"

—Sandy Daniels, President and CEO,
Johnson County Community Foundation

"As we write this we are in Tanzania visiting the site of a soon-to-be-established model girls' secondary school which may well change the way that young women in Africa are educated and prepared for leadership—and this project could not be happening without PVF's being willing to support truly innovative ideas. As usual, PVF does with ease what others consider to be difficult."

—Peter and Jane Carpenter, longtime PVF donors

"Bill Somerville's instincts for serving the poor come from years of work conducted out of the office and in the community. I have yet to go to a program that is up and running for the poor that Bill hasn't already visited. Site visits by anyone from a foundation are rare, particularly in our area of work; site visits from executive directors of foundations are unheard-of. Bill's enthusiasm is contagious and necessary when life gets hard—and life can get hard. For Bill, grant-making grows out of being with and responding to the poor, and I see PVF not as a funder, but as a co-worker and partner."

—Larry Purcell, Founder, Catholic Worker House, Redwood City

"I cannot begin to tell how much I was moved by Bill Somerville's work and the lives of the people it touches every day. He opened my eyes to the other safety net beyond the better-known safety net, and how trust is the true agent of change and progress."

—Gabriel Garcia, M.D., Professor of Medicine, Associate Dean of Medical School Admissions, and Peter E. Haas Director, Haas Center for Public Service at Stanford University

Grassroots Philanthropy

Field Notes of a Maverick Grantmaker

Bill Somerville with Fred Setterberg

Foreword by Colburn Wilbur

Heyday Books, Berkeley, California

Library of Congress Cataloging-in-Publication Data

Somerville, Bill.
    Grassroots philanthropy : field notes of a maverick grant-maker / Bill Somerville with Fred Setterberg ; foreword by Cole Wilbur.
       p. cm.
    ISBN 978-1-59714-084-3 (hardcover : alk. paper)
    1. Endowments--United States--Management. 2. Non-profit organizations--United States--Management. I. Setterberg, Fred. II. Title.
    HD62.6.S62 2008
    658.15'224--dc22   2007030435

Front Cover Art: © Andrey Armyagov
Back Cover Photo: Paul Bishop, Jr.
Cover Design: Leigh McLellan Design
Interior Design/Typesetting: Leigh McLellan Design
Printing and Binding: McNaughton & Gunn, Saline, MI

Orders, inquiries, and correspondence should be addressed to:
    Heyday Books
    P. O. Box 9145, Berkeley, CA 94709
    (510) 549-3564, Fax (510) 549-1889
    www.heydaybooks.com

Printed in the United States of America
on 50% post consumer waste recycled paper ♻

10 9 8 7 6 5 4 3 2 1

Contents

Acknowledgments

ACKNOWLEDGMENT is a way of recognizing special people who help to make things possible, such as this book. I am indebted to Albert J. Horn, a friend and advisor for the past thirty-three years, to Colburn Wilbur for his friendship and astute advice over the years, and to my staff, Moira C. Walsh and Dawn Hawk, for their support and assertiveness in getting things done.

Dedication

*Ruth Chance was my mentor. She was the second
executive director of the Rosenberg Foundation in
San Francisco and possibly one of the most diligent and
delightful people in the foundation field. I miss her.*

Foreword

by Colburn Wilbur

IN THE FOLLOWING PAGES, Bill Somerville provides us with ideas, suggestions, and experiences that would help any foundation, large or small, experienced or new, and any employee or board member. Bill is known as a maverick and a revolutionary grantmaker because he trusts people and acts quickly. Ask almost anyone in the low-income communities in which Bill Somerville has worked, and they will tell you a story about how a modest grant helped them to accomplish something special that changed and improved the lives of people in that community. Providing juvenile court judges, school superintendents, and principals with a fund from which they can help young people purchase glasses, new clothes, bus passes for commuting, or special training can make a major difference in whether a young person succeeds or not. An excellent judge of character, Bill knows whom to trust, and he is willing to provide funds even when the results are not immediately obvious: a grant of less than five hundred dollars brought together a motorcycle group and the city police force in a Bay Area town for a Sunday baseball game and barbeque, allowing these two groups to understand each other and develop a lasting cooperative association.

Bill believes that foundations can accomplish far more than they do currently by following some basic, commonsense suggestions. These include spending the time to know the community in which one provides grants; learning who the key players providing community services are; finding the best people (not necessarily the best known), and trusting them—and sometimes taking a risk in supporting them. Bill spends time visiting the communities in which he works, asking many people whom they admire and trust. This effort often turns up effective people who, though they may not be well known and are not necessarily those who direct the largest agencies, can make a difference in their communities.

Since the 1970s, The David and Lucile Packard Foundation has worked with Bill, first at the Peninsula Community Foundation (and its predecessor, the San Mateo Foundation) and for the past seventeen years at Philanthropic Ventures Foundation. I was the CEO of the Packard Foundation for twenty-three years, during which time the Packard Foundation also supported Bill's consulting to over three hundred community foundations in the U.S., Canada, and England. When I retired as CEO in 1999, I was asked to join the Packard Foundation Board of Trustees. Shortly after that I also joined the board of Philanthropic Ventures Foundation, so I have known Bill and been learning from him since 1976. Whether the Packard Foundation's total grants were $600,000 (1976) or $500 million (2000), it was often more effective and efficient to support Bill's efforts in low-income communities than to try to make the grants ourselves. I greatly admire his skills at reaching community activists, teachers, artists, judges, government employees, and many others.

It is important for foundations to try to ensure that their grants are spent in a way that will improve our lives in some respect. Yet too many foundations have designed a grantmaking process that is complicated and bureaucratic, and takes far longer than necessary. Great ideas often need to be supported quickly, and Bill has designed a system to provide grants to teachers and artists within twenty-four hours. Even when a grant is large and the situation complicated, Bill has spent enough time learning about needs and opportunities in advance to act quickly. He is a master at providing excellent grants in a short time, getting the money where it is needed.

Bill is very good at helping people think about how to be more effective. His approach is not "this is what to do": he mentions possibilities and allows the listener to think about them. He respects the judgment of his grantees while trying to be helpful. Having a world of experience developed over his thirty-three years of philanthropy and a wonderful imagination, he helps to develop programs while leaving the credit to the grantee.

Bill Somerville is the CEO of a medium-sized foundation that uses its money wisely. However, the suggestions provided in this book would help trustees or directors of smaller foundations, and it should be read by individuals and corporate giving program officers. It would also be very helpful for program officers from larger foundations working in low-income areas, either urban or rural. Too many of us become so much involved in the process of grantmaking that we do not pay enough attention to our goals of helping individuals and whole communities to prosper. This book is full of ideas that will help any grantmaker; here is a voice in philanthropy that should be taken seriously.

Colburn Wilbur
August 2007

1 Philanthropy's Untapped Potential

How Grassroots Grantmaking Can Breathe New Life into Foundations

ONE MORNING, just before sunrise, I found myself prowling across the loading dock of the South San Francisco produce market, searching for damaged fruits and vegetables. My partner on the loading dock was an ex-priest helping the local soup kitchen. Philanthropic Ventures Foundation had paid for the truck he used each morning to stock up on food too bruised or discolored to be sold. This time around, I asked to tag along and lend a hand.

It was a glorious day. I could smell the ocean and feel the bay breeze in my face, and I thoroughly enjoyed throwing my back and shoulders into the work—I was happy to be away from my desk, yet still engaged in the business of philanthropy. Soon, the morning got even better. We scored several large crates of sweet yellow onions destined to fill the soup kitchen's lunch pot for the coming week.

The soup kitchen fed six hundred people each day. Over the past few years, I'd eaten there at least twenty times. I'd seen how, for many of the folks at society's margins, it served as the one stabilizing factor in their lives, alleviating the utter despair that accompanies an empty stomach.

We loaded the heavy crates of onions into the back of the truck. I gazed at the truckful of food and thought once again that I must be one of the luckiest men alive. I was standing exactly where I needed to be—learning precisely what was required of me as a human being, and as a philanthropist. The bay breeze, the sound of forklifts and rattling hand trucks, the voices and faces that I'd never encounter inside a foundation conference room—all this was a part of my continuing education as a grantmaker.

For the past three decades, I've had the privilege of working as a foundation executive. In many ways, it's been an intensely gratifying experience, filled with opportunities for meeting terrific people, learning from them, and helping whenever possible to nudge the world towards a more just and equitable future. Frankly, I can't imagine a better way to have spent my life.

But that morning at the produce market, standing on the loading dock, thinking about the deep and pervasive needs facing American society, I also had to ask myself a troubling question: *Why aren't we—the entire philanthropic sector—doing a much better job?*

I know that some people in the field today will argue that foundations are accomplishing tremendous things, with the sector growing smarter and stronger as it swells in number, assets, and professional staff. Unfortunately, I don't think the record bears out such optimistic assessments. Over the course of this book, I will say much more about philanthropy's shortcomings. But for the moment, I simply want to acknowledge the enormous potential that does exist for foundations to transform American life.

Foundations today possess a dazzling amount of wealth—some sixty-seven thousand institutions have assets in the billions—and the numbers are growing. This fortune constitutes the raw capital for building a better world.

As foundation trustees and staff, we enjoy almost complete freedom in deciding how this money will be spent. Unlike professionals employed by the private or public sectors, we must answer neither to the demands of stockholders nor the inconstant will of the electorate.

Our activities are constrained by a bare minimum of governmental regulation and red tape. And since the people who start foundations are by definition America's wealthiest and most privileged individuals, with access to the nation's opinion shapers and policy makers, we are in a position to function with few restrictions on our creativity.

Perhaps most important—but practically never acknowledged—is the fact that those of us working for foundations pass each day with the luxury of a fiscal safety net afforded no other set of institutions or individuals. Whether our performance as grantmakers proves inspired or inept, our endowments provide us with permanent employment and a guaranteed annual income.

Given these advantages, it would seem logical that foundations should be accomplishing things nobody else in American society would even dare to attempt. But collectively, we have fallen far short of this mark.

Why?

I believe that our lackluster performance can be attributed to five flaws:

Paper-laden Bureaucracy: Philanthropy is erected upon a trough of waste paper. Consider the zillions of pages of grant proposals hammered out over the years. Think of the mountains of evaluations, budgets, letters of decline and approval, and gilt-edged annual reports. Imagine the frustration of nonprofits as they attempt to weave their way through the maze of application procedures, and their fury when their letters, phone calls, and e-mails don't get returned promptly—or at all—by staff who are steadily sinking in their own pools of paper. Despite our freedom to construct institutions that make sense and serve people's needs, foundations more often emulate the worst aspects of big government, with cumbersome regulations, endless forms, and arcane bureaucratic procedures.

Slow, Stubborn, and Unresponsive: Foundations move like molasses. Everybody knows it's true. And there's no excuse for it. Grant proposals take months to be reviewed, even when the answer turns out to be an unambiguous **no**. Checks require weeks or longer to reach the hands of cash-strapped nonprofits. When we could choose to be quick, deft, and decisive, we more frequently lumber along like sleepy giants.

Aversion to Risk: The thought of failure terrifies most funders. With almost nothing to lose, grantmakers persistently embrace safe and predictable projects instead of untested, but promising, new ideas. They confuse bold action with recklessness. Imagine if this attitude prevailed in other aspects of American life. There would be no cell phones, no computers, no man on the moon, no Declaration of Independence, and perhaps no Columbus sailing across the perilous seas. Great achievements almost always involve calculated risks.

Problem-centered: Many foundations dedicate themselves to the ceaseless study of problems instead of generating new ideas to solve them. Indeed, funders frequently confuse their expression of concern with the far more demanding task of taking action. Too often, the result is the costly underwriting of yet another "official report" that inevitably gets filed away and forgotten. By defining the world exclusively in terms of its faults and inadequacies, funders drag down their own efforts and siphon off the entrepreneurial energy of the true problem solvers—our nonprofit collaborators.

Passivity: Foundations set up shop and then wait for the deluge of grant applications to come pouring in. Staff seldom leaves the office, unless it's to confer with other funders. Executives and trustees would rather insulate themselves from the nonprofit sector than wade into its midst to locate potential collaborators. Instead of taking action, we become mired in reaction.

I wish I could say that these five flaws have diminished in recent years. In truth, they have only become more deeply entrenched. Over the past decade, new foundations have been established at a furious rate, with most fledgling philanthropists understandably looking to their more experienced peers for guidance in forging their own approaches to grantmaking. As a consequence, the five flaws have been driven even deeper into the fabric of philanthropy.

For the Love of Humanity

THE FLAWS THAT plague philanthropy are serious. But they also can be solved—if we set our minds to the task.

Over the years, I have worked with many wise and dedicated people in both the philanthropic and nonprofit sectors. I've learned from their insights and actions, and I've added my own thoughts whenever the lightning bolt of a bright, useful idea has managed to strike. Together, we've launched countless new programs leading to tangible and sometimes very substantial results. Once again, I want to stress that the nature of this work has been collaborative, our efforts bound together by a "love for humanity," literally. *Philanthropy*: *philos*, love; *anthropy*, mankind.

And that's a wonderful starting place. But when it comes to changing the world, sometimes even love isn't enough.

We also need a diagram of how philanthropy works, what's gone wrong, and an action plan to correct it. We need examples, success stories, and frank appraisals of our failures. We need to engage the face, voice, and most of all, the human heart of philanthropy.

It's in this spirit that I offer my five-point program for enlivening and reforming philanthropy:

- Locate outstanding people doing important work
- Move quickly (and shred paper)
- Embrace risk
- Focus on ideas instead of problems
- Take initiative

The second half of this book will illustrate exactly what I mean by each of these principles. My advice and examples are aimed at small family foundations, community foundations, staffed foundations, and foundations with motivated trustees willing to handle some of the tasks that good grantmaking demands. The grants under discussion will prove modest in size, bypassing efforts at structural change and the reshaping of public policy. Instead, we will focus on concrete benefits to local communities achieved by delivering the right amount at the right time—a strategy frequently overlooked.

But first, I want to step back and speak more personally about what philanthropy has meant to me throughout my life, and why I feel so strongly about changing its fundamental approach.

2 One Man's Route to Philanthropy

How I Got My Start in the Foundation World

MY PHILANTHROPIC CAREER is rooted in the San Francisco Bay Area's busy, bustling, idea-rich nonprofit sector of the 1960s. After earning my graduate degree from the School of Criminology at the University of California, Berkeley, I spent the next fourteen years working as the program administrator and then executive director for a procession of fledgling nonprofits variously dedicated to children's welfare, race relations, prisoner rehabilitation, job development, and other issues linked to the quest for social justice. Although I didn't realize it at the time, this experience would shape my appreciation of philanthropy's potential—and set the direction for the rest of my life.

Like most people in the nonprofit sector, I had to contend with all the usual disappointments and obstacles associated with seeking foundation grants. I routinely juggled a host of applications, forms, and reports utterly unrelated to my organization's mission or the quality of our work. I waited in vain for foundation staff to return phone calls. I discovered that my most enthusiastic and well-reasoned pleas for support would often be met with aloof indifference, which had the effect, though unintended, of making me feel small, insignificant, and expendable. Worst of all, I watched promising ideas die on the vine for lack of a few sustaining dollars.

In other words, I couldn't have received any better preparation for my subsequent career as a foundation executive.

I knew exactly what not to do.

So when I took my first foundation job at the San Mateo Foundation some thirty years ago, I swore that I would never behave in the manner that I had routinely encountered as a grantseeker.

I treasure the years I spent working as a nonprofit staff member. I firmly believe that direct personal experience within the sector is invaluable for anybody making decisions about where grant money will go. In fact, I credit the insights and experience I gained in the nonprofit world, along with the unavoidable bumps and bruises acquired there, with paving the way for my best efforts in philanthropy. But to be fair, I must also admit that I came to the foundation world with some distinct personal advantages.

To begin, I grew up poor. My mother's family fled Oklahoma during the Dust Bowl of the 1930s, lured to California by the promise of steady work. Mom's parents divorced, and she spent time in the fields picking cotton along with her six siblings. At sixteen, Mom dropped out of high school, pregnant with her first child, and she married Dad, who had also quit school—in the fourth grade—to help feed his family. Dad eventually learned the hot-lead printing trade and my folks opened a small print shop in San Francisco. Our family was definitely "low income." And although I have never mentioned this fact to any of my peers in the foundation world—I blanch even now at the disclosure—as a child, I had rickets.

School also proved tough for me at first. I was hyperactive, dyslexic, and God knows what else. My attention in class often shattered like glass, scattering everywhere but where it should have been. Today I would be called learning disabled. Back then, school just felt like an endless procession of failed tests whose only explanation rested with my own intellectual inadequacy. Today I understand something about poor children struggling to grasp the basics of reading and writing in many of the public schools I now routinely visit as a grantmaker. In many ways, their experience reflects my own.

Fortunately, my parents set a courageous example. I watched Mom and Dad striving to lift our family out of poverty. If one strategy didn't work, they tried something else. Failure simply marked the starting point for their next effort. They never gave up.

Even as a child, I recognized my parents' extraordinary qualities—their eagerness to learn, their infectious curiosity, the way they were seized with a hunger for justice. To them, the inequities of this world proved vivid and undeniable. My parents encouraged me to emulate their example by giving my best to whatever endeavor I undertook. If I failed the first time out—and I usually did—Mom and Dad bucked me up and sent me back out to try again. That's the strategy that finally got me through school. I learned early that nothing succeeds like persistence.

I also learned at a young age to take risks. I remember being seventeen years old and weeping to my mother that I wasn't smart enough to go to college. Although nobody in our family had the slightest notion what college might entail or how it would change my life, both my parents urged me to give it everything I had. So I applied to UC Berkeley. To my astonishment, they accepted my application. "Now tell me again," asked Dad, staring at that unexpected letter of acceptance. "Why are you going to college?" I answered honestly: "Darned, if I know."

I think Mom and Dad understood that with an education I might be able to pick up where they had left off; and they instinctively knew that with an education, I might be able to play a modest role in narrowing the gap between America's aspirations for justice and equality and its inconsistent record of results.

I entered a new world as an undergraduate at UC Berkeley. I can still picture myself on campus—a blue-collar kid, and proud of the fact, thrashing my way through this elite bastion of the educated middle class. Some days, I felt convinced that I didn't belong at Berkeley and would probably fail, but I vowed to go down swinging. I worked as hard as I knew how, and gradually I saw myself advancing, learning, succeeding. I had been given a chance, and I gripped it with both hands. But I never forgot that my leap forward in life was made possible by the sacrifice of my parents and the generosity and good sense of the citizens of California, whose tax dollars had opened a great public university's doors to an ordinary kid like me. I owed them all a great debt—more than I would ever be able to repay. But I wanted to try.

After graduation, I completed a two-year hitch in the Navy and then returned to help my folks with their printing business. But I had acquired a taste for education, and I soon returned to UC Berkeley as a graduate student in criminology. At Berkeley, I started working with a series of social programs that aimed to benefit the poor and disenfranchised—people I knew because I had grown up as one of them. I thrilled to the notion that somebody with a good idea, and sufficient skill and determination to carry it out, might change the world. As a staff member at Stiles Hall on the UC campus, I labored alongside an energetic board to set up a program linking undergraduate tutors with inmates at San Quentin prison. Then I helped found the School Resource Volunteers to dispatch some of the brightest and most committed students on the UC campus to assist poor kids in the Bay Area's inner-city schools. These experiences established the trajectory for the rest of my life.

Just as important, I also met a wonderful woman who would prove to be my mentor and role model once I entered the foundation world.

Ruth Chance served as the program officer for San Francisco's Rosenberg Foundation, a pioneering institution in the field of child welfare. Ruth's genuine "love of humanity" marked her as a philanthropist in the true sense of the word. Her example as a tireless, frequently inspired grantmaker profoundly shaped my own conception of what foundation work could and should be—given sufficient reserves of courage, energy, and humility.

I recall one of our first meetings, back in 1962. Ruth and I sat in my Volkswagen bus on a sweltering summer's day outside a junior high school in Berkeley that I wanted to help. Perspiration trailed down our faces, but we kept talking with a kind of furious mutual absorption about the potential of School Resource Volunteers, then in its earliest stages. "But *who* will run the program?" demanded Ruth, who was considering a start-up grant. "That's my essential concern." For the first time, I grasped the importance of this seemingly simple question. Without good people, great ideas rate merely as words. Management plans, organizational charts, even bulging bank accounts—none of these things guarantee success. *People* run programs, for good or ill, and the quality of their skills and commitment inexorably shape the results. I never forgot this discussion. To this day, the centrality of outstanding people in the pursuit of great achievements remains one of the tenets of my own work in philanthropy.

I learned a great deal more from Ruth over the years. I saw that as a foundation officer she ended up saying "no" to grant applicants far more often than "yes." Yet she never diminished anybody in the process of making her decision. Ruth respected people as a matter of policy and personal conviction. She kept her promises. She admitted when she didn't know something and she took pains to educate herself about as wide a world as possible—it was just part of the job. She combined modesty about her own role with a ferocious ambition for her cause and the groups she funded. And she exhibited a marvelous sense of humor that delivered her to the quick of knotty problems and sustained her balance through a host of challenging personal relationships.

"Suspicion of one's own motives," the philosopher Bertrand Russell once observed, "is especially necessary for the philanthropist." Ruth exemplified the hard-won self-knowledge implicit in this tenet.

Other people in both the nonprofit and philanthropic worlds also taught me a great deal. In the 1960s, the San Francisco Bay Area seemed a veritable idea factory. Some of these big ideas eventually produced impressive results—I'm thinking about Head Start, state programs to provide health insurance to poor children, the rise of community foundations. Others foundered, as inevitably happens when people take risks. But a spirit of experimentation prevailed, and a heightened sense of possibility enlivened the era. My early experience with people compelled to put their ideas into action spawned my lifelong faith in the transformative power of the imagination. And like my parents, I was—and remain—willing to accept the occasional failure, even a gargantuan blunder or two, if it marks the continuing road of thoughtful experimentation leading eventually to success.

The Future of Philanthropy

For almost two decades now, I have had the privilege of directing Philanthropic Ventures Foundation (PVF), headquartered in Oakland, California. Our small office lies a proverbial stone's throw from Berkeley, where I grew up, received my formal education, and continue to live. (In fact, my own family occupies the same house my parents bought decades ago to raise us kids in.) And professionally, armed now with experience and ideas, I have the opportunity to address a portion of the injustice that I first witnessed as a child.

In the world of philanthropy, PVF ranks as a small institution. Our annual grantmaking is under $10 million. Our staff consists of three full-time employees and one part-time assistant. We pride ourselves on dismantling bureaucracy, acting with decisive speed, and striving always to immerse ourselves in the heart of community life.

Over the course of this book, I will describe our work in detail. Most pointedly, I will attempt to show how PVF addresses the five flaws now undermining philanthropy—while offering a model that can be adapted by foundations of far greater (or lesser) size throughout the country.

For now, I want to take the observer's role and talk from the perspective of a grantmaker with more than three decades of experience about what I see happening today in philanthropy.

Let's start with the good news.

We are now anticipating an unprecedented generational transfer of wealth in America. Over the next half-century, trillions of dollars will be handed down from parents to children and then on to grandchildren. Whatever the final figure, the sum will prove staggering, with estimates at the low end amounting to four times the present size of the American economy.

What will the new rich do with their wealth? Only four options exist:

1. Spend it all in an orgy of conspicuous consumption

2. Invest it wisely to make more money (or lose it by dribs and drabs or in one fell swoop...)

3. Pass it down to the next generation, and risk turning them into idlers

4. Become a philanthropist

The last option has a long and distinguished pedigree in America. Andrew Carnegie, the most influential philanthropist of the past two centuries, once declared, "The man who dies rich, dies disgraced." By the end of his life, Carnegie had proven true to his word, disposing of 90 percent of his fortune through an imaginative network of foundations and trusts. His projects were bold, their impact sweeping—from the Carnegie public libraries, whose doors still swing open throughout American cities and small towns, to the expansion of our greatest universities.

But even Carnegie couldn't have imagined the philanthropic potential of the next fifty years. Indeed, some scholars estimate that foundations could be granting up to $200 billion a year by the mid-twenty-first century, or ten times what they gave in 2001.

To my mind, this prospect of an enormous swell of foundation giving is both exhilarating and troubling.

The reasons for celebration seem obvious: with great fortunes at our disposal, we can accomplish great deeds. What's the downside? My concerns should be apparent to anybody taking an honest look at the record of conventional foundation grantmaking.

I believe that only the most cockeyed optimist would suggest that the next wave of foundation directors and trustees will reinvent themselves in a spirit of daring, risk, and imagination that runs counter to conventional practice—unless they are urged, cajoled, enticed, instructed, and inspired to do so.

In other words, I worry about the foundation world producing much, *much* more of the same.

How can the staff, directors, and trustees of philanthropic institutions apply the kind of energy, strategy, and creativity that will reap the most significant results?

That is the question I will attempt to address throughout the rest of this book.

3 Getting Started

(By Getting Our Facts Straight about Foundations)

BEFORE WE LAUNCH into our discussion about how to improve and enliven foundation grantmaking, I want to explore some common and widespread misconceptions about our sector.

Let's start by admitting that most Americans don't know the first thing about philanthropy.

Then again, how could they? Not a single mass market print journalist is assigned a full-time beat to cover the foundation world. Television reporting remains negligible—at best, reduced to announcements of ambitious funding initiatives sponsored by the larger institutions (at worst, the minute-long teasers that broadcasters periodically trot out about some local funder who may have wandered awry of its fiscal responsibilities). From the great stages of public life—the governor's mansion, the Senate, the White House—we almost never hear a knowledgeable word uttered about philanthropy's practices, problems, or promise (except perhaps an announcement that the government is pulling out of funding this or that enterprise, and it will now be up to foundations to pick up the slack...). Altogether, it's a mind-boggling omission. Despite our size, wealth, influence, and potential, philanthropy is absent from the national conversation.

Of course, those of us in the field must assume some of the responsibility. One reason for the pervasive disinterest in our activities involves the language that now saturates our sector. *In-puts, through-puts, benchmarking, strategic planning, endowments, privatizing*: foundation-ese jargon that suggests to the uninitiated that philanthropy resides solely in the realm of tedious bureaucracy.

And that's dead wrong. Philanthropy is a fascinating pursuit. It's the stuff of dreams made practical, a lever that can move the world. Philanthropy is a subject about which I remain unequivocally and unapologetically *passionate*.

Yet I don't often sense that passion when I speak with my colleagues. And I certainly don't hear it when I attend the usual round of lectures at national conferences or when I try to plow through treatises and monographs that replace the genuine expression of human feeling with the terminology of management theory.

For me, philanthropy *is* an emotional subject. And I think that our manner of speaking about philanthropic efforts should reflect our emotional depths. We should strive to project the excitement of philanthropy, inspiring other people to launch their own grantmaking programs—not least, by showing how much satisfaction and (dare I say?) *fun* our work affords us.

If I may be a bit provocative here, I also want to suggest that the cloudiness of our role in American life may actually suit many people in the foundation world. After all, if nobody is paying attention, we can keep on doing what we've always done. We don't have to worry about public expectations because the public has no expectations.

Indeed, the little that most people do seem to believe about philanthropy usually turns out to be wrong.

Among the most common misapprehensions:

- **Philanthropy is just a fancy word for charity.** Far too many times, I've heard people say, "Oh, I could easily be a 'philanthropist.' Anybody can give money away." But in professional foundation work, nobody *gives* away anything. Ideally, we *invest* in outstanding people undertaking important work. The task—and the subject of this book—is to learn how to *find* those people, *engage* their energy and imagination, and *negotiate* a successful grant. And while we're on the subject, let me state that even the word "grant" is misleading. Foundation executives are not members of an aristocracy, deigning to hand out boons and benefits to a motley array of subordinates. This kind of attitude (all the more powerful for its unstated and conscious grip) poisons relationships and undermines everybody's dignity. Our collaboration with nonprofits should result in something closer to a good-faith contract with the expectations on both sides spelled out candidly, lucidly, and briefly.

- **Foundations are simply a tax dodge for the rich.** Would our nation serve as home to more than sixty-seven thousand private foundations if the federal tax laws did not encourage their establishment? Absolutely not. America's tax code—to put a complex matter rather baldly—discourages the redistribution of wealth, at least as it's been undertaken by the social welfare states of Europe. Instead, we reward the rich of our country with substantial tax savings—around 30 percent—when they place their fortunes at the disposal of private foundations dedicated to public benefits. As a result, America has a far more vigorous independent sector than any nation on Earth, and many more grantmakers. But to dismiss foundations as a complex maneuver for wealthy people to "pass Go" without paying taxes is to ignore both the personal motivations behind the impulse of generosity (see "Seven Reasons Why People Give," page 21) and our national legacy. America may be the most radically individualistic of societies, but it is also the world's most associative. "As soon as several of the inhabitants of the United States have taken up an opinion or feeling which they wish to promote in the world," wrote Alexis de Tocqueville in 1835, "they look out for mutual assistance; and as soon as they have found each other, they combine. From that moment, they are no longer isolated men, but a power seen from afar, whose actions serve for an example, and whose language is listened to." Foundation resources fuel America's continuing urge for mutual aid and association.

- **Foundations pour their resources into fighting injustice and ameliorating the plight of the poor.** I wish I could say this assumption is correct. Over the years, I have heard many people suggest that the great foundations must naturally devote their energies to aiding our society's most vulnerable citizens, while addressing the conditions that breed poverty, ignorance, and despair. In truth, most foundations shy away from activist grants for fear of the controversy they might stir up. The statistics on national grantmaking bear witness to our sector's reluctance to confront the inequities of American society. According to a 2005 report issued jointly by Independent Sector and the Foundation Center, the largest U.S. foundations allocate only 11 percent of their giving "for structural changes aiding those least well off economically, socially, and politically." Where does the rest of our money go? By far, the lion's share of institutional giving winds up in the coffers of the great universities, national mega-charities such as the Red Cross and Salvation Army, and local cultural mainstays—symphony, opera, and ballet. As a tonic, we should all remember the words of Martin Luther King, whose Southern Christian Leadership Conference, along with other key organizations of the civil rights movement, received crucial support from several brave activist funders in the 1960s. "Philanthropy is commendable," wrote King, "but it must not cause the philanthropist to overlook the circumstances of economic injustice which make philanthropy necessary."

- **Foundations are run by well-trained professionals impeccably educated in the practice of philanthropy.** What constitutes a profession? We assume that professionals possess a college degree related to their field, pass an entrance exam, acquire certification, and take required annual training courses. In philanthropy, none of these conditions apply. Foundation executives usually vault into their offices from positions of power and esteem in academia, public service, or the nonprofit sector. Almost nobody walks onto the job with previous training—if only for the reason that training opportunities remain scattered and sparse. (While university nonprofit management courses continue to proliferate, the cultivation of foundation leadership takes place at what can only be charitably described as an avocational level.) To a degree unimaginable in business, government, or almost any other profession, foundation staff learn their trade by plying it—usually blindly at first. In recent years, standards have emerged within the field, but they tend to cover grantmaking behaviors and ethics, such as rules for how long it should take to return phone calls and why one must avoid self-dealing. The quality of grantmaking—the heart of our enterprise—remains a vague matter of personal and institutional whim. Indeed, no sanctions exist against mediocre performance, and no baseline of effectiveness has been established by which the novice or veteran grantmaker can measure performance and determine if he or she is doing a good job. To put it perhaps a bit too bluntly: too many of us with too much wealth and power know too little about our jobs and have too little motivation to learn more.

Oddly enough, there is also a bright side to this "unprofessionalism." It gives us an opportunity to peel away the thin skin of careerism and the sector's exclusive old boys' club attitude in favor of a more passionate, open-hearted, and open-minded stance.

I advocate that we look at philanthropy as a *vocation*, with those of us professionally engaged answering to a *higher calling*. I don't particularly care how any individual might characterize the source of this calling. It might be a love of humanity, a devotion to God, or a conviction that justice must be served. The point remains: we need to lift foundation life out of the realm of everyday prosody, while injecting into our mission and daily activities a sense of urgency, passion, and poetry.

Three Unanticipated Obstacles: Money, Power, and Privilege

UNFORTUNATELY, our nation's ignorance about philanthropy extends beyond the general public to include many people within the foundation world. Most critically, we fail to recognize that the chief benefits of working in a foundation—money, power, and

Seven Reasons Why People Give

Emotion
"My wife died in that hospital; my brother died of cancer—thus I am motivated to give to the hospital building fund or the annual drive of the American Cancer Society."

It Sounds Good
"I am persuaded by the speaker, public relations professional, or direct mail solicitation that my money will be well spent."

Recommendation
There is a saying in philanthropy that people don't give to organizations or causes, they give to people: "I trust you. You recommend a charity. I write my check."

Prestige
Public recognition of a donor's generosity motivates both the direction and size of a gift.

Tax Considerations
Wealthy donors usually get substantial tax deductions for their giving, and this fact figures prominently in the advice given by their financial counselors.

Coercion
"When we pass the plate, we hope everyone will be generous in their support," suggests your minister. "Last year we had 100 percent contributions by the employees and we hope for the same this year," says your boss. Mild and heavy-handed encouragements to give often reap results.

Default
"I don't know who to give my money to. I guess I'll give to the same groups I've always supported."

privilege—also rank as the three greatest obstacles to doing a good job. This paradox is written into the DNA of every foundation, and it's our responsibility to be aware of the complications so that we can neutralize their deleterious effects.

Money: As a foundation staffer, you now stand as the gatekeeper to a fortune. You literally have your hands on millions, if only for a few minutes, when you're writing the checks. It's easy to embrace this role with ferocious, self-deluding pride. After all, everybody would rather identify with wealth than poverty. But keep in mind: *it's not your money*. You only work here. Nevertheless, your proximity to wealth will always be the first fact noticed by the rest of the world, and it will alter your relationships, personal as well as professional. Whenever you encounter trusted colleagues from the nonprofit world—even people you consider to be friends—they will inevitably glimpse the glow of the money behind you. It's simply unreasonable to expect anybody to gloss over its presence. Likewise, you may ignore it only at your own peril.

Power: Money translates directly into power, whether you desire to exercise it or not. An old joke in philanthropy states that once you start working for a foundation, you will never again have a bad meal or a bad idea. People will twist themselves into knots to please you—even if that means acceding to your shallow insights, baseless opinions, and bad advice. Can you blame them? You hold the purse strings, and if you wish to be humored and charmed, then most people will happily go along. In this regard, you can level only one defense: don't take yourself too seriously. Someone once sent me a card that read, "Angels can fly because they take themselves lightly." I like that. It's easy to get dragged down by one's self-importance. And who is going to tell us when we're about to plummet to earth? Certainly not the grantees who depend on us.

Privilege: Generally, people working in foundations don't possess a great deal of firsthand knowledge about the poor and desperate. And they certainly won't learn anything by hunkering down in their offices. But that's exactly what most foundation executives do. And when they finally step outside, they tend to gather among their fellow philanthropists. The shoptalk that results ultimately proves pointless because it lacks candor. Very little self-criticism gets ventilated at professional meetings; we air blandishments such as "we should be more open and responsive" but never quite get down to the nub of how that can be achieved. One effect of philanthropy's insularity is that we fail to develop the tough hide that most people in public life must acquire. We become hypersensitive to criticism, and on the rare occasions when it's fired in our direction, we panic, deny, or capitulate. It's an absurd situation. If there's anybody in American society who should feel secure, it's foundation executives. But when I ask people in the nonprofit sector if foundation personnel take more risks than most people, everybody laughs. Experience, sadly, tells them otherwise.

Bolder, Braver Philanthropy

NONPROFITS SUM UP the imperfections of foundation staff with a single unflattering word: *arrogance*. While this is certainly a damning appraisal, I think to focus on the unpleasant personal characteristics of some foundation staff actually covers up a far worse systemic flaw. The real problem is not that some foundation executives may simultaneously prove haughty, timid, callous, and hypersensitive. Rather, it's that the philanthropic sector as a whole fails to embrace the virtues of courage, imagination, curiosity, and flexibility, and fails to feel profound gratitude for the opportunity to play a potentially transformative role in American society. Yes, I know: individuals create institutions, and any criticism we may harbor about the performance of foundations finally comes down to the attitudes and actions of staff and trustees. But we also must remember that institutions serve as the crucibles that form—even reshape—individuals, and that's particularly true for institutions of enormous wealth, power, and prestige.

If we hope to resuscitate the wasted potential of the foundation world's vast, independent, and largely unregulated wealth, we must begin everywhere at once—altering our philanthropic institutions by emboldening the individuals at their helms.

4 The Search for Outstanding People

Principle #1:

Locate outstanding people doing important work

"Behold, I do not give lectures or a little charity,
When I give I give myself."
—*Walt Whitman*, Song of Myself

NOTHING IS MORE IMPORTANT to the success of a
voluntary program than its people.

You can choke off the cash flow to a trickle, stick the office in
some decrepit hole-in-the-wall, lay siege to daily operations with
every imaginable distraction and obstruction—but if the program is
led by outstanding people, the effort can still succeed brilliantly.

That's why I look to excellence in leadership as the first require-
ment for any program that I am seriously considering funding.

Perhaps this seems obvious. In truth, most foundations place
too much stock in the organizational apparatus *encasing* people: the
five-year plans, annual reports, and most lamentably, grant applications. In effect, these materials erect a paper wall around the individuals charged with getting the work done. They obscure the personal element that lies at the heart of all social progress, and foster

the illusion that organizations somehow run of their own accord, without the benefit of human inspiration and guidance. But plans are merely words committed to paper. Even after reading the savviest, best-constructed grant proposal, I still want to know: *Who is going to make this plan work?*

- Are the people in charge tough, resilient, courageous?
- Do they possess the necessary skills?
- Have they succeeded in the past?
- Do they have clear ambitions for the future?
- Are they capable of recognizing their mistakes and changing course?
- How do they deal with failure?
- Are they utterly convinced of their work's importance?
- How long have they been on the job?
- How long are they committed to staying?
- Is there an heir apparent to the top leadership on staff?
- How is staff morale? Is there any data on turnover?
- How often does the board meet? How many members attend regularly?
- Does the board trust the executive to lead the organization?
- What do the people served by the organization say about its leaders?
- What do other professionals in the field think about the staff?

In short, I focus on the human side of nonprofit enterprise, searching for commitment, skill, vision, and integrity.

Plus one other essential: *passion.*

Nonprofit leaders require huge reserves of vigor and stamina to fuel their efforts. Anything less will end in wilted programs and

The Qualities of Outstanding Nonprofit Professionals

Humor	Outstanding people balance their seriousness about work with an ability to laugh at almost anything—including themselves.
Ambition	Outstanding people burn with an unquenchable longing to make good things happen.
Optimism	Outstanding people view seemingly hopeless situations as issues waiting to be resolved.
Vision	Outstanding people recognize possibilities that remain hazy, opaque, or invisible to others.
Realism	Outstanding people maintain a sense of proportion, concentrating on the work at hand rather than inflated daydreams.
Instinct	Outstanding people learn to trust the good sense of their gut feelings and intuition.
Consistency	Outstanding people stick it out for the long haul—which can mean years, decades, or even the course of an entire lifetime.

a dead shell of an organization. But there's another reason why I seek outstanding people as collaborators: they inspire me. I find my enthusiasm renewed every time I meet an individual determined to make the world a better place. In fact, I've come to picture effective leaders in terms of three incendiary varieties:

Sparkers, who generate ideas

Igniters, who turn ideas into programs

Burners, who keep programs percolating within an effective organization

All three kinds of leaders contribute to nonprofit success. But rarely does a single person fit into all three categories. More often, I'll run into a *Sparker* who can *ignite* his field with well-designed programs, or an *Igniter* who can keep her organization *burning* steadily through times of want, crisis, or opportunity. My goal is to meet as many as possible, and find ways that we can work together to make a better world.

People, Not Paper

MOST FUNDERS wait for good people to find them. That's the logic underlying the grant cycle: we ensconce ourselves in our comfortable offices, hoist a flag saying we're open for business, and wait for the proposals to come sailing in. And they do—in immense, paralyzing abundance. Soon, we're chained to our desks, sifting through a mountain of paperwork, straining to determine from the oblique evidence of several printed pages which projects might conceivably further our goals as funders. Then we read, read, and read some more...

The grant cycle is one of philanthropy's sacred cows, and I have any number of bones to pick with it. To begin, we can point to the waste of time, the tedium that attends the protracted routines of proposal submission and review, the exaggerated claims that it encourages applicants to make, the attitude of overwhelmed disdain that too often characterizes the stance of funders. But my chief criticism is that the grant cycle impedes, diverts, or outright obstructs the search for outstanding leaders. It substitutes paper for people.

Indeed, even the most compelling proposals seldom address critical questions about the character and commitment of the people in charge. The best proposals may reflect nothing more than superior writing skills and an ability to anticipate whatever pleases the funder. In most cases, the rigid format and lifeless language that typify grant proposal-ese obscure the personal qualities of our potential collaborators and mask the human face lurking behind each request. What's more, many of the best people in the voluntary sector actually shun the grant-seeking treadmill. Experience tells them that foundation philanthropy can absorb their time and effort in a bureaucratic rigmarole that often fails to yield commensurate results. They put their energy elsewhere.

But it's not just the grant applicants who suffer. The grant cycle also turns our work as funders into a stultifying routine when it could and should be exhilarating, adventurous, and deeply satisfying. The proposals piling up on our desks make us slaves to the grant cycle and isolate us inside our offices. As a direct result, we have neither the occasion to meet outstanding people in the field nor the opportunity to cultivate the skills needed to recognize them when they do come our way.

What's the answer?

We must dismantle the bureaucracy that imprisons us and step out into the world that lies beyond our office doors.

Leaving Your Office to Get the Real Work Done

RECENTLY, I asked the executive of an established foundation how often she managed to get out of her office to meet people working on the kinds of projects she hoped to fund.

"Thirty-five percent of the time?" I wondered.

"Certainly not," she said, looking offended—as though I had accused her of neglecting her real duties.

"Then a quarter of your time?"

"No, no, no," she said.

"Fifteen percent?"

She shrugged sheepishly, realizing now what I was driving at. "Maybe ten percent of the time," she admitted. Then she pointed to the stack of paper rising from the surface of her desk. "It's my guilt pile," she explained, "my to-read pile. It just gets bigger and bigger. How can I leave when there's so much to do?"

I mention this exchange because it reflects a common misconception about where our responsibilities as funders truly lie. How can we indulge the *luxury* of getting out into the field, we ask ourselves (with just a hint of self-pity and self-aggrandizement), when so much *work* remains on our desks?

Of course, this question misstates the situation. We should be asking, *How can we make more time for philanthropy's real work: the continuing investigation of our community, its problems, its potential, and most of all, the outstanding people with whom we should be making common cause?*

Let's be frank. Most foundation staff do not get out into the field even ten percent of the time. When they do leave their offices, it's usually not to meet nonprofit folks in unfamiliar settings, but to gather with other funders in all the usual places. As a result, many grantmakers inhabit a hall of mirrors, an echo chamber. They know too much about the culture of foundations and too little about the world.

Before I begin to sound like a scold, I want to admit that I struggle with this dilemma just like everybody else. Some mornings, I glance at my calendar and I realize that I have a nine a.m. appointment twenty miles away, on the other side of the San Francisco Bay, and I just groan. I mentally list all the reasons not to go: the awful commute, the probability of rain, all the letters I need to answer, all the phone calls I really should make. Sometimes I'd just rather hunker down in my office and let the day take me wherever it may.

I resist the temptation.

I fish my keys out of my pocket, trudge over to the car, and force myself into the driver's seat. Once I turn the ignition and head out towards the highway, my reluctance vanishes like smoke. I know that I am taking the first liberating step towards what almost always turns out to be—at the very least—an interesting adventure. Oftentimes, it proves to be a great deal more.

Thirty years of experience in philanthropy have persuaded me that exploring the world that surrounds our foundation is more exciting, stimulating, informative, productive, and fun than most duties I'll dispatch back at my desk. Most important, it's the only way I can meet the people best suited to become collaborators.

Then why do most of us experience such difficulty when it comes to freeing ourselves from the office routine—even for a few hours each week?

1. **Inertia:** We fall prey to the psychological manifestation of physical law: bodies at rest want to stay put. It's just human nature to resist pulling ourselves out of our comfortable chairs—and our cozy roles as grantmakers— to venture someplace new.

2. **Delusions of a grander view:** Spend enough time inside a foundation bureaucracy, and you'll start believing that from your elevated perch you can spy all that's taking place around you. You confuse a generous scope of vision with the daily onslaught of e-mail, telephone calls, and grant proposals.

3. **Fear:** Life inside a foundation can be safe, predictable, untroubled by the harsher complications of human aspiration, rivalry, conflict, disappointment, and failure. The world outside is incomparably vast, unpredictable, and frightening.

4. **Unwillingness to surrender our positions of privilege:** As long as grantseekers flock to our doors, we remain in control. We decide who and what to support, and when to review proposals, write the checks, and stick them in the mail.

Out in the world, we can be met with disinterest, disrespect, ignorance, and even hostility.

5. **Lack of models:** Isolation is self-perpetuating. Most of us have never met a foundation director who spends even a quarter of her time outside the office, and so we never suspect that the strategy can be effective.

6. **Fatigue:** Even when you do manage to drag yourself off to interesting places, you'll still need to dispatch fifty other duties back at your desk. Over time, it's just easier to surrender to routine. Indeed, maintaining an active schedule of firsthand community research requires constant vigilance.

Mired Down in the Muck of Meetings

ONE OTHER FACTOR inhibits the outward urge, but it's not a matter of psychology. Rather, it's the fact that foundations hold too many meetings. We excel at meetings. We drown in meetings.

I want to propose a radical alternative: don't go. Try it as an experiment for three months. Resolve to skip any meeting, particularly with other funders, functionaries, or government bureaucrats, whose purpose seems to you less than essential. Then use that time to get out of your office and talk with people in the nonprofit sector who you would not otherwise meet.

I have kept my own vow of shunning superfluous meetings for many years now, and I don't believe that I have suffered as a result. When I have college interns working for our foundation, I often send them to gatherings which, for reasons of collegial courtesy or financial practicality, I cannot ignore, and then we later debrief. As a result, everybody is happy. The meetings get along just as well without me (some would say better…) and I am free to devote my time to talking with the people in our community who would never have been invited.

The Slow (but Steady) Education of a Foundation Executive

I FUND PEOPLE, not proposals. It's a principle I embrace with all my heart, and over the years it has produced wonderful results with some remarkable collaborators.

Ah, very well, you say, but how do you recognize those people? Where do you find them? How can you tell the real item from the faker, the worthwhile risk from the foolhardy fly at the moon?

I'll be the first to admit that it's not easy. The process of identifying outstanding people takes time, persistence, a willingness to make mistakes, and enough resilience to render you open, even eager, to try again.

Yes, but how do you *begin*?

My advice: follow your nose and just dive in.

Let me give you an example.

Twenty-five years ago, I got a call from one of my foundation's major donors about a priest she had heard speaking the previous Sunday at her church. Father Larry Purcell worked with teenagers at Juvenile Hall, and he related to the congregation harrowing stories about the crimes these kids had committed, the neglect they had suffered—and the potential each possessed for personal and civic redemption. I asked our donor what excited her about Father Larry's sermon. She explained that it was the sense that he was utterly dedicated to improving the lives of these kids who most people feared and shunned.

I telephoned Larry that afternoon.

"What can we do for these kids?" I asked.

"Buy them a jukebox," he said. Life at Juvenile Hall, Father Larry explained, was boring, endless, pointless; the most frequent diversions were fights. "Buy them a jukebox because nobody else will, and it might make a difference."

Now, I'll admit that this request might have turned out to be a stupid idea with absolutely no effect. It could have even backfired somehow, embarrassing us all. But I had a sense that Larry knew what he was talking about, and so I took a risk. I spent a few days digging around, and I eventually located a very colorful character who sold old jukeboxes out of a warehouse. He wouldn't take my check, wouldn't deliver the goods, demanded cash in an envelope, and told me I had to haul the jukebox to Juvenile Hall in my own Volkswagen van. But the kids got their jukebox, and it served them well.

It also launched my philanthropic relationship with Father Larry Purcell—who soon left the priesthood and threw himself into work with what I would come to recognize as his customary determination and enthusiasm. Larry told me from the start that he wasn't interested in applying for a grant. He didn't operate a 501(c)(3) nonprofit organization, and he had no interest in starting one for the sake of foundation support.

"I don't believe in foundations," he told me. "I don't believe in grants. I believe in people power." Larry's disdain for conventional grantmaking bordered on belligerence, but I didn't take it personally. I saw that he was an interesting guy—a little quirky, but exceptional in his commitment, energy, and resourcefulness. Over the years, I've come to realize that many of the best people can at first seem a bit eccentric. It's part of their outsider's stance that enables them to defy convention and blaze new trails. But back then, all I knew was that Larry seemed to me somebody worth knowing.

Larry soon opened a house for what he called "throwaway youth." The kids had to abide by a contract for academic achievement and involve themselves in community work—all part of Larry's plan for preparing them to take their places in the world as responsible adults.

Over the next few years, I'd get calls from Larry whenever he saw ways that we might collaborate. One morning, he told me about a teenager ready to get out of a California Youth Authority facility, where he had been sent after shooting, and missing, his abusive father. In jail, the kid had trained to be a refrigerator repairman. Larry located a mom-and-pop store that agreed to hire him but couldn't pay a full salary. Our foundation underwrote his apprenticeship. After a few months, the kid stopped coming to work and then disappeared from town. "Strike one," I told Larry. "We missed on that one. But we'll try again." Today I'm not sure that we did miss. The kid eventually showed up on a local construction crew. Perhaps our intervention at a critical moment in his life had made the difference in keeping him out of further trouble. Anyway, it had seemed worth the gamble.

My point is this: I would have never known about any of these funding opportunities if it hadn't been for Larry. But the Larry Purcells of this world won't necessarily seek you out.

You have to find them.

And once you've found them, you need to cultivate a relationship based on mutual trust, respect, and understanding. More than once, I have had to persuade some of my unconventional nonprofit collaborators, like Larry, to accept the money our foundation offered.

Is this grantmaking as usual?

Of course not.

It's much better. The emphasis on working with outstanding people—be they eccentric iconoclasts or not—has two extraordinary virtues that are absent in conventional grantmaking. First, your new collaborators usually turn out to be long-term renewable resources. Outstanding leaders are, by definition, highly committed folks, capable of enduring effort and great flights of imagination. They will probably remain in your community for many years, drawing your attention to a variety of projects and people that might have otherwise escaped your notice.

Blazing New Trails with Intuition and Trust

MY RELATIONSHIP with most of the people we fund depends on two qualities we don't talk about much in philanthropy: intuition and trust.

Intuition, I believe, is largely a matter of openness to one's own experience. When I *feel* something about a new project, place, or person, I am instantaneously tapping the accumulated experience of fifteen years' work as a nonprofit director and thirty-plus years in philanthropy. But I don't let my intuition lead me into snap judgments. Rather, my gut feelings tell me to pay attention because *something I don't yet understand* is happening, and it's my responsibility to learn more. Intuition is my alarm clock; it wakes me up to possibilities worth pursuing. It compels me to start asking questions.

Trust is equally important. Indeed, I believe that trust is one of philanthropy's most underutilized tools: the lubricant, if you will, that over time allows our relationships to expand with greater complexity and ambition and without needless chafing, conflict, wear, or exhaustion.

Of course, many grantmakers withhold their trust, fearing that they'll be taken for naive do-gooders—easy marks among the predatory and unscrupulous. I think this reluctance to exercise trust is a sign of weakness, not strength. It reflects a lack of self-knowledge, a fear that one's experience in the world is too limited to distinguish the inspired from the incompetent, the openhearted from the hustlers.

I make it a point when I meet somebody new to extend my hand in trust, expecting that the other person will respond in like manner and good faith. I don't worry about rejection, misunderstanding, or manipulation. After all, the handshake is just the beginning, a sign of my willingness to join others as part of a team. Time will tell if my initial trust is justified. Until then, I've lost nothing, and I have everything to gain.

How does trust unfold in the real world?

I'm thinking now about the St. Francis Center in Redwood City, run by some Catholic activists in the neighborhood. From the beginning, trust got the relationship moving: Larry Purcell made the introduction, and I felt that anybody he recommended was at least worth an hour's visit.

On my first trip to the St. Francis Center, I spent a few hours talking with its director at the time, Sister Monica, about the economic conditions plaguing the surrounding Latino immigrant neighborhood. I liked what Sister Monica had to say; she wasn't a dreamer, ideologue, or fanatic, but a smart, compassionate, and practical person. She personally knew most of the families in her small neighborhood, and she understood the forces that mired them in poverty. Sister Monica subsequently retired, and Sister Christina replaced her—another knowledgeable and committed person.

When Sister Christina urged me to read *Nickel and Dimed*, Barbara Ehrenreich's chronicle of struggling to make ends meet through a procession of low-wage jobs, I extended my trust another small leap and devoted several hours to the task. The book impressed me. Most strikingly, I recognized it as a reflection of Redwood City's barrio.

"What can we do to help?" I asked Sister Christina.

"Start a school," she immediately shot back.

Why a school? Sister Christina explained that a small elementary school could profoundly improve the prospects for a dozen families in the neighborhood by concentrating on the children's education while simultaneously advancing their mothers' earning power.

The school soon opened with twelve children.

The teacher, who Philanthropic Ventures Foundation (PVF) funds, emphasizes reading, writing, and math—gateway skills for future achievement. In eighteen months, the children's reading level rose two full grades. Their mothers—most of whom spoke no English—volunteered one day each week in the classroom, studied English with volunteer tutors, and mastered basic computer skills. More than eighty volunteers, mostly seniors, helped distribute food and clothing and labored in the community garden that has blossomed across the street.

Over the past few years, I've visited St. Francis Center at least twenty times and I am always impressed by the joyous enthusiasm of the students, coupled with the order, discipline, and gracious good manners that characterize their school. Most recently, I listened to the children discuss their favorite artists: Picasso, Pollock, Chagall, Van Gogh, Rivera. They talked about their ambitions for college— an expectation constantly reinforced by their teachers, and now, by their parents—and their aspirations to one day become doctors, lawyers, veterinarians, car mechanics, and visual artists.

After the first conversation I held with Sister Christina, I could never have dreamed of what is being achieved today in this classroom. But I trusted that something of value was likely to come into existence—given what I knew from firsthand experience with the people involved. Trust allowed PVF to help build a small, important neighborhood institution that is as effective as it is beautiful to behold.

Sharpening Your Skills to Find Outstanding People

IDENTIFYING outstanding people is a skill that depends almost entirely on practice. To be sure, instinct paves the way—but as I've said, it, too, relies on a bedrock of experience. In the end, you've simply got to root yourself out of your office on a regular basis and put yourself through the paces in the field.

That said, I want to recommend several practices that I believe can add to your knowledge of your local community while strengthening your ability to recognize its resident Sparkers, Igniters, and Burners.

- **Study the local news:** I read seven newspapers regularly, and I always keep my keenest eye focused on local reporting. What I'm after is the mention of interesting people and programs whose names are new to me. If you don't have time to leaf through the newspaper yourself, assign an intern to the task, or subscribe to a clipping service.

- **Develop specialties:** Years ago when I worked for UC Berkeley, I visited 112 high schools over a very short period of time in a quest to recruit more minority students. To this day, I can enter a school and immediately get a feeling for the place. Do students and teachers converse between classes or does an air of sullen disengagement prevail? Does litter clog the hallways and graffiti mar the bathrooms? All these little things add up, indicating the quality of an institution and the people who run it. I've come to recognize the significance of these details only because of the great number of hours I've logged on school grounds.

- **Make yourself (slightly) uncomfortable:** I'm often struck by the reluctance of my colleagues in the foundation world to move beyond their comfort zones. As a group, we simply aren't used to having our authority, motivation, or worldviews questioned. Yet when I'm out in the field, it's precisely these kinds of challenges that I'm seeking. If I go too many days without feeling slightly out of my element—even a bit anxious in the face of the unfamiliar—then I know I'm stuck in a rut of my own making. At that point, I strike out in new directions, knowing that I stand a better chance of learning something unpredictable and valuable.

- **Get the entire staff involved:** At PVF, everybody on staff assumes some responsibility for grantmaking. That means we all have to schedule time out in the field, multiplying the possibilities for meeting outstanding people in places new to each of us.

- **Cultivate a reputation for curiosity:** As you start to spend more time in the field, word of your interests and attitude will precede you. Folks will start telling you about issues, efforts, organizations, and people beyond your usual acquaintance. Your curiosity will prove a magnet for the unexpected.

Stringers and Other Strangers

MANY FOUNDATION executives naively believe that they already know all the important players in their town. But even small communities are complex social hives, with far more taking place than any one person can absorb. To complicate matters, dedicated nonprofit leaders may shrug off distractions, such as the cultivation of public honors and the company of movers and shakers. Isolated within their work niches, they may labor productively, but invisibly, for years.

That's why I have come to use "stringers." The term derives from the newspaper business: a stringer is a kind of a freelance reporter covering a particular beat, such as the courts or schools. I turn to stringers of various sorts to locate outstanding people throughout the San Francisco Bay Area who spend their lives accomplishing important work in relative anonymity.

Journalists often make the best philanthropic stringers. After all, they're in the business of digging up news in remote corners of the community. Indeed, nothing is prized more highly among reporters than knowing about interesting things that have escaped everyone else's notice.

I make a habit of asking the newspaper and TV professionals I meet about stories they're covering, people who have impressed them lately, individuals that they think I might want to learn more about. Several years ago, I was talking with a newspaper reporter about a story she had recently filed concerning an ex-gang member with a car detailing business who hired other young men seeking an alternative to gang life. I later called up the car detailer and visited his shop, and together we devised a way to add more young men to his training program by underwriting his liability insurance coverage.

Other kinds of stringers can also provide useful leads. If I want to know who is shaking up the criminal justice system, I talk to judges, probation officers, and police. When I'm trying to look more deeply into creating jobs in low-income communities, I'll speak with businesspeople, labor organizers, or a university economist studying the region. Sometimes I'll ask a person with no prior investigatory experience—but whose intelligence and motivation I trust—to spend some time digging around his community to identify *anybody* attempting *something interesting*. I deliberately frame my request in vague terms, and then stand back to see if my candidate has the makings of an effective stringer. In the past, I've found adept sleuths in the Junior League, high schools, and among an energetic corps of retired people. In every case, the point has been to expand the breadth and depth of my own foundation's vision by borrowing the eyes of numerous well-placed observers.

Another variation on the stringer is to ask one outstanding person about the colleagues she considers to be peers. After all, outstanding people cannot waste time with sloggers and obstructionists; they seek out like-minded partners in order to advance their own agendas. Whenever I meet a person whose work truly impresses me, I always query them about coconspirators, competitors, and professionals in other fields who have impressed them. Or conversely, whenever I encounter an important but dysfunctional institution, such as a badly managed school or a hopeless tangle of municipal bureaucracy, I ask around about any exceptional people burrowed within who are known for getting things done, whose word can be relied on, who habitually exhibit energy and ambition. Dedicated people exist within even the most inept institutions—and oftentimes the worse the organizational pathology is, the more evident the rare occasions of excellence will be.

Site Visits in Pursuit of Outstanding People

IDENTIFYING POTENTIAL collaborators is merely step one. Now it's time to meet them.

When I learn about an individual of interest—whether from news reports or personal recommendation—I telephone as soon as possible and introduce myself. I explain who I am and what our foundation does, and I ask if I can drop by in a day or so for a conversation about their operations.

Once again, I must emphasize that what I'm looking for is an *individual* of extraordinary commitment, character, skills, and motivation. All else—ideas, programs, organization—hinges upon the presence of the outstanding person.

Before my visit, I take an hour or so to review whatever written materials I may possess. They might include newspaper articles, position papers—or just a few notes I've scrawled to myself at an earlier point to remind me why the person interests me. I usually keep it to just a few pages—the less reading, the better. To be sure, I want the facts. But I prefer not to invest too much time digesting somebody else's views. My aim is to remain grounded in reality and open to new experience.

More important than reading about the person or agency I'm about to visit are the questions I plan to ask. I always write a list of specific inquiries to serve as the blueprint for our conversation. If the visit proves intriguing, I'll inevitably come up with another dozen questions during the course of an hour's conversation. Later, when I return to my office, my original list will also remind me about any misconceptions I may have harbored prior to our meeting. The distance between what I imagined and what I discover often proves instructive—not least by pointing out my own assumptions, prejudices, and gaps in knowledge.

Upon arriving at the meeting, I settle down to business immediately. Occasionally, I'll visit an agency without an appointment—particularly if it seems important to get a feel for the place without any preparation on my behalf. In either case, the shape of the visit remains much the same. I stress that I'm there for a working session, not a social occasion. I let everybody know that I don't want to waste their time any more than my own.

If I'm visiting an organization that has already submitted a grant proposal, I'll usually open the conversation with a gambit that goes something like this:

"Thank you for taking the time to talk with me.

"This is your session as much as mine, and part of our job today is to strengthen your proposal as much as possible.

"As with all proposals, there were questions that came up when I read yours, and I want to directly ask you about them.

"If you feel that I have misread or missed your main points, please tell me.

"If there are any key omissions in your proposal that now occur to you, let's talk about them, too.

"In short, I'd like us to anticipate any concerns that might arise for the members of my grants committee—because if we don't answer these questions, they'll either vote no or postpone their decision…"

If the organization has not already submitted a proposal, I have a bit more freedom in orchestrating our conversation. Generally, I'll start by asking about the organization's mission and activities. Most executive directors will immediately launch into their "elevator story"—the two-minute spiel they learn to pitch in the time it takes to ascend from the ground floor to a foundation's fourteenth-story executive suite. I don't resist. This conventional take provides me with the basic facts, evokes the organizational self-image, and demonstrates the director's ability to conceptualize and then sell his program. But that's just the beginning. If I'm intrigued by what I'm hearing, I will move the conversation along by asking:

- **How do you know you're having an effect?** (I'm open to a variety of proofs: studies, testimonials, a persuasive articulation of evidence that would have never occurred to me. Mostly, I'm listening to the manner in which the person makes his case.)

- **Is anybody else doing similar work in your community?** (If not, that's interesting. If so, and they don't know about it, that also tells me something I need to know.)

- **Why do you work here?** (If I'm talking to somebody who turns out to be a mere job holder, then I know our relationship will quickly reach its limits. I'm looking for someone who knows in her guts why she sticks with a difficult position. I'm searching for commitment that can keep an organization running for years.)

- **What do you envision for the future?** (There's no right answer. But I do want to hear whether folks are thinking about alternatives, possibilities, dreams. I subscribe to the biblical injunction "Where there is no vision, there is no hope.")

I suppose I could come up with a dozen other questions that have over time served my curiosity and our foundation's interests. But they would be *my* questions; your own investigations will demand a unique route of inquiry. What I'm arguing for here is an unconventional spirit of openness, an equality of purpose in which the funder surrenders his usual advantage in order to engage with a potential collaborator in the frankest possible terms. I am advocating for humanity, honesty, and humility in grantmaking.

After an introductory conversation, I'll usually ask to be shown the premises. I'm a great believer in conducting site visits by wandering around. The most obvious advantage is that I'll see with my own eyes whether the organization does what it claims. Are kids pouring through the front door for music lessons? Does the classroom look like a place of learning and excitement? Are the phones ringing? How does staff interact with clients? What is the physical condition of the building? If I see something that alarms or confuses—say, the doors are still locked at nine a.m. and no clients whatsoever ever seem to arrive—then I'll also have the opportunity to ask why. I work hard at this point to withhold any judgments about the program or people. It's not yet the place or time. I'm still endeavoring to reconcile the theoretical (the elevator story) with the actual (what I see happening before my very eyes). I need to keep my mind clear to recognize any differences between the two.

I also take the opportunity to ask "dumb questions."

"Why do teenagers start taking drugs?"

"How do homeless people end up on the streets?"

"Does it really matter if the snail darter goes extinct?"

"Dumb" questions are really honest inquiries—the novice's declaration that he plans to cast off prior assumptions and misconceptions and head straight for the basics. It's not easy to ask the dumb question. It cuts against the grain of our self-images as educated professionals, the people with the checkbooks—and by implication, the answers. But we shouldn't let ourselves get caught in the need to appear informed when we're really standing at square one.

Your foundation may fund programs involved with education, health care, the environment, homelessness, drug addiction, and fifty other issues. It's simply not possible to be up to speed on them all. But it is advantageous and often necessary to admit your ignorance and ask the beginner's question. Oftentimes you'll get an answer that will surprise you and suddenly make possible unpredictable good things in the future.

I strive to limit my visits to an hour or less. I realize that the agency people are keenly hoping for our foundation's support; they'd tolerate my loitering in their offices forever, if I wanted. I try to be a good guest and leave on time.

At the end of the visit, I'll often ask for the names of three or four professionals familiar with the agency and its leaders. I'll telephone these folks the next day from my office to solicit their thoughts. If I'm showered with superlatives about the people and program, then I'll push a bit harder to hear about any weaknesses. It's surprising how often references will take this cue, change course, and respond more candidly. I'll then add their comments to the brief notes I've taken regarding the visit, file them all away for future reference—and hope that when I return to them some days or even weeks later, my impressions will prove accurate and fresh.

I have just summarized the usual course of my site visits. And yet there is one powerful aspect of the experience that I haven't touched on.

I'm talking about the salutary role of emotion.

Site visits frequently turn out to be very moving experiences. When I meet people who have dedicated their lives to helping the poorest and most vulnerable among us, I cannot respond in a purely intellectual manner. I'm an emotional person. I know that about myself, and that self-knowledge helps me gauge my reactions when I'm out in the field. To be sure, emotions can color, even distort, our judgment as grantmakers. But in most cases, I don't think that's what foundation executives have to worry about.

I contend that philanthropy affords too little importance to human feeling. Please understand, I am in no way a sucker for a sob story. I abhor the waste that goes with "rescue funding"— grants tossed to a sinking ship of a program that will only stay afloat long enough to ask for help once more. But I do, with all frankness, frequently find myself moved to tears by some of the people I meet in the nonprofit sector.

Much of what I see—in the best cases, where outstanding people tackle terrifically difficult issues and produce worthwhile results—is beautiful. It's the stuff of democracy in action: smart, independent, ambitious individuals working together in pursuit of a more just and equitable society.

Our task is to find these people, open our hearts to the possibilities they present, and join forces with them to change the world.

Three Good Reasons *Not* to Leave Your Office

ALTHOUGH I REMAIN firmly convinced that most grantmakers spend far too much time chained to their desks, I also recognize that some site visits do more harm than good. Among the kinds of firsthand investigations to avoid:

1. **A pleasant amble around the nonprofit neighborhood:** You've met the director of a local nonprofit at a schmoozing event for funders and prospective grantees. She seemed like a nice enough person, and you recall some interesting things she had to say about her recent vacation in the Everglades. You decide to drop by for a chat. What's the harm?

   Or to put it less charitably: You're bored. You have some time to kill. You're unprepared for the rigors of a genuine site visit. You don't mind wasting everybody's time. You haven't considered the prospect of raising expectations in regard to funding that may not material-ize. You have the power to go wherever you want and nobody's going to criticize your decision—at least not to your face.

2. **The payback:** One of your board members, an old col-lege pal, or your brother-in-law drops an unmistakable

hint that your presence at his favorite nonprofit would be greatly appreciated. You already know that your foundation cannot and will not consider the organization's application for any number of ironclad reasons, but you arrange a site visit just the same. A bad situation only grows worse, as your arrival stirs unrealistic hopes and prepares the ground for a sense of betrayal.

3. **The expert arrives:** You show up at the nonprofit's doorstep in order to offer the benefit of your expertise—be it how to run a program or muster an effective board. Heads nod, notes get taken. Everybody seems delighted to listen. But when you finally leave, the beleaguered staff of the put-upon nonprofit know they've been had.

   Grantmakers who dole out advice on their site visits misunderstand their role. You're not there to instruct, guide, or inspire. Your task is more challenging: you need to soak up everything of importance about the project, premises, and people in a preposterously short amount of time. In a word, you're there to *learn*. Of course, as your relationship with a grantee matures, occasions may arise when your perspective will prove helpful and even desired. But never on the "first date." The occasion is too freighted with expectations. In hopes of getting funded, potential grantees may heed your advice, even if it proves wretched. And you will have only filled your ears with the sound of your own voice, thereby failing to note the more subtle music of the unfamiliar organization.

A Final Plea for People

ACCORDING to a recent study by the Bridgespan Group, in Boston, the difficulty that nonprofits have in attracting, recruiting, and retaining qualified leaders will only grow more pronounced over the next few years. In the coming decade, nonprofits will have to recruit sixty-four thousand new leaders—roughly two and a half times the number currently employed—to make up for staff who retire or leave senior leadership positions for other endeavors.

"The amount of social impact a nonprofit organization delivers is primarily dependent upon the capability and performance of the people in that organization," concluded Thomas J. Tierney, the report's author and the chair and cofounder of Bridgespan. "Results are a 'who thing.'"

I couldn't agree more.

I also believe this looming crisis on the nonprofit horizon encourages—indeed, compels—equally dramatic changes within the foundation world.

The most important action we can take to strengthen the nonprofit sector—and to ensure the integrity and effectiveness of our democracy—is to place much more emphasis as grantmakers on finding and supporting outstanding people. I like to imagine a philanthropic sector where foundation executives get out of their offices and into the field at least 30 percent of their work time. Frankly, that would mark a revolutionary change in philanthropy. And it's a change that's entirely possible for all of us.

5 Grantmaking with Speed and Grace

Principle #2:

Move quickly (and shred paper)

"Generosity lies less in giving much than
in giving at the right moment."
　　　　　　　　　—*Jean de La Bruyère*

GOOD PHILANTHROPY is good timing.

You can fund outstanding people undertaking important work—but the results will often prove disappointing unless you dispatch your grant *at the right time.*

Yet for most foundations, the right time is preposterously slow in arriving—six, nine, sometimes even twelve months after receiving a proposal. Indeed, foundations are famously poky institutions. They bring to mind Samuel Johnson's timeless definition of a philanthropist as "one who looks with unconcern on a Man struggling for Life in the water and when he has reached ground encumbers him with help." Johnson's quip referred to the ponderous deliberations of eighteenth-century English aristocrats who considered themselves responsible to no one but themselves. Unfortunately, the characterization still holds true for today's funders—despite an explicit duty to render service to the public with all due speed.

It's a frustrating situation. Funders expect their nonprofit partners to be fleet, nimble, able to turn on a dime. They, on the other hand, make grants at their own convenience—and then they call it a schedule.

Why do foundations chug along so slowly?

- Unnecessary paperwork clogging the arteries of their bloated bureaucracies
- Sheer terror at the possibility of making a mistake

Let's consider the bureaucratic morass first.

Most foundations fund paper, not people. Instead of combing their communities for outstanding collaborators, they wait for people to find them. No, not people—but proposals, which hardly rates as the same thing. By relying on the grant proposal as the means of identifying worthwhile projects, funders lapse into "factory philanthropy"—an endless, exhausting routine in which the process of proposal acceptance, review, and response emerges as the institutional product. Even the best funders frequently lapse into this routine. The proposal review process is the default position in philanthropy.

Of course, many nonprofits eventually cultivate (or hire) the skills necessary to become adept at the grant game. The staff immerse themselves in the exacting application requirements and with time they learn to craft appealing plans for worthwhile projects—at least, on paper. But for other organizations, the application procedure proves so onerous that the grant becomes a reimbursement for the time it took to apply. More than once, I've heard nonprofit executives complain, with only the faintest exaggeration, that they must spend five thousand dollars' worth of effort to secure a thousand-dollar grant. Can you imagine a more impractical or wasteful arrangement? If foundations plied their trade in a free market with genuine competition for the nonprofit partnerships they need to justify their existence, most would go broke.

Unavoidably, the weight of hundreds or even thousands of proposals pouring in each year requires the construction of a supporting bureaucracy. Consider all the paper generated by the review process: the application forms; multiple copies of proposals; letters of decline, deliberation, and award; program officer summaries; executive recommendations; grants committee reports; board dockets; financial bookkeeping; and eventually, formal evaluations of everything alluded to in all the aforementioned papers…To carry this load, many foundations adopt an organizational model that owes more to the paper-ravening apparatus of the federal government than the sleek design expected of the best nonprofits. In sum, the paper, procedures, and Byzantine bureaucracy separate the grantmaker from grantseekers, distance foundation staff from the community at large, and slow philanthropic progress to a crawl.

Which brings us to the second reason why foundations plod along when they could move swiftly: paralytic fear.

Most grantmakers dread the prospect of publicly making a mistake. In order to shield themselves from embarrassing recriminations for the project that fails, the organization that goes belly up, or the crook who absconds with the money, funders coat their operations with a thick layer of protective documentation—supporting materials, such as board bios, annual budgets, audits, five-year plans. But such paper-thin armor provides almost no real defense against the possibility of project mishaps or the rare scoundrel with his hand in the cash box. What all these documents actually cover is the rear end of the grantmaker.

Please understand, I take due diligence seriously. I just don't believe that the legalistic formalities of paper shuffling achieve this goal. Many foundations harbor the illusion that the more procedures and record keeping they impose on the grantee, the greater due diligence they've achieved. Not so. Due diligence is a process, not a pile of papers destined to languish forever in the file cabinet. Due diligence emerges over time from the effort of finding outstanding people, cultivating trust, and clarifying the aims and design of a prospective project. Due diligence isn't certified; it's excavated, mined from extensive experience in the field. Over the years, I have found that due diligence is only possible when I wrench myself out of my office to thoroughly familiarize myself with a potential grantee. It hinges upon my intuition, my expectations for creativity from all parties, my knowledge of the social context of the issue at hand, and my willingness to take risks.

Of course, there is one more reason why most foundations prove so leisurely in dispatching their duties: nobody demands that we move any faster.

Recently, one of the largest foundations in the San Francisco Bay Area announced that it had pared back its proposal review process from nine months to seven. The announcement was met with praise by the philanthropic community. What it deserved was a howl of derisive laughter—which is precisely what you heard from staffers of nonprofits when they gathered privately among themselves.

Everybody knows foundations take far too much time to review and respond to proposals. Yet few people enjoy the leverage to challenge the status quo. Nonprofit fundraisers may mutter to one another about institutional arrogance and grind their teeth all night in dismay. But they still have to line up in the morning to ask for support, while pretending that the timing makes sense. Nationally, there will never be a public hue and cry for foundations to act in a prompt manner, because the inner workings of philanthropy remain invisible to most people.

I'm afraid that it may all come down to us—grantmakers and grantseekers who care enough about the vitality of the independent sector to risk the censure of our peers and the support of conventional funders. Together, we have to demand that foundations respond to requests with speed, dispatch, and cheerful alacrity.

Most important, those of us with some means at our disposal must put into practice the time-saving methods for grantmaking that have already proven to work.

The Power of Paperless Giving

I HAVE AN INTENSE aversion to pointless paperwork. I don't like to read, write, or even file away fifty-page grant applications, reports, or evaluations. And I know I'm not alone. Most of us in philanthropy regard paperwork as a nuisance and think of "bureaucracy" purely in a pejorative light—all with good reason.

At Philanthropic Ventures Foundation (PVF), we take pride in unshackling ourselves from both burdens. We conduct our work at a swift pace, but we avoid franticness. We consciously reject the self-important rushing around—the culture of virtuous busyness—that so often stands as a substitute for genuine achievement in many sectors of American society.

Then how do we operate?

Whenever possible, we aim for paperless giving.

I realize that in philanthropy's paper-laden culture such a notion may sound preposterous. But please remember that only a few years ago, it seemed revolutionary to ask airline passengers to fly without paper tickets in hand. Nothing changes…and then everything changes overnight.

Our own brand of paperless giving rests on two assumptions:

- Program officers need to devote at least 30 percent of their time to exploring the community in order to locate outstanding people to fund.

- The best way to free up program officers' time is to reduce paperwork.

Let me explain how this works in practice by pointing to an example of near-paperless giving—our "immediate response grants."

Fax Grants for Teachers

SEVERAL YEARS AGO, one of our donors handed us a check for one hundred thousand dollars and asked us to spend it on education. Although California once led the nation in the quality of its public schools, the state has in recent times plummeted to the bottom in terms of spending, test scores, and other signs of academic achievement. In many large cities, public schools have resegregated along racial and economic lines, with the middle class opting for expensive private schools and the poor and recent immigrants occupying the crumbling public infrastructure. In our own region, two of the largest districts were taken over by the state because of fiscal mismanagement. The threat of teachers' strikes has become routine. Dropout rates in many schools exceed 50 percent. In short, education has reached a crisis.

In the face of such daunting problems, what could we do with a mere hundred thousand dollars?

We knew that this sum could not address the large structural inadequacies, such as low teachers' salaries or the deteriorating physical state of many campuses. And we certainly didn't want to enmesh ourselves in the public school bureaucracies that had already proven unresponsive on many levels. So we tried to think strategically, drawing upon the experience we had accumulated over the years from visiting hundreds of schools and speaking with thousands of teachers.

We knew that the classroom supplies and discretionary funds that had once been available during California's golden days of public education were now in short supply. If teachers desired to try something new with their students, or even pursue the ordinary course of their daily lesson plans with all the necessary materials, they often had to pay for them out of their own pockets. Field trips proved a prohibitive luxury.

Our solution: ask the teachers what they needed in terms of supplies and travel funds, and immediately put the money to pay for it in their pockets. Thus was born a strategy that we've continued to use in a variety of circumstances—the immediate response grant. Or as our local teachers began to call this particular effort: fax grants.

To begin, we sent a one-page flyer to each of the Bay Area's forty-seven thousand teachers, encouraging them to ask for up to five hundred dollars to underwrite a field trip or purchase science equipment, art supplies, or whatever else they deemed necessary. The teachers then faxed our office a one-page request on their school letterhead, cosigned by the principal, along with documentation of purchase costs, such as copies of catalog pages.

We reviewed each proposal as it reeled off the fax machine. Some days, they arrived nonstop. We quickly approved the good grants—the vast majority—and we mailed checks out to the teachers within twenty-four hours.

The teachers soon wrote back to tell us how their projects had fared. And at that point, we knew that we had stumbled upon an efficient means of directing resources where and when they were needed:

- At Live Oak School in Santa Cruz, Arin Murrell, a first-grade teacher, purchased science texts, prisms, magnetism kits, and magnifying glasses. "My students use these materials on a daily basis," she told us, "and they will continue to support learning in my classroom for years."

- At Fox Elementary School in Belmont, third-grade teacher Sarah Smith received $175 to pay for makeup for the opera her students staged each year. In the past, Smith had covered all the costs herself.

- Second-grade teachers at Christopher Columbus School in Daly City took their children to the San Francisco Zoo. "Many of our students had only seen these animals on television or in photographs," wrote teacher Lisa Ramson. "Having the opportunity to see the animals with their own eyes was an unforgettable experience for each of them."

- Jim Broadstreet, a sixth-grade science teacher at Highland Elementary School in Richmond, requested $472 to purchase fossils to teach his students about paleontology. After immersing themselves in the subject, his sixth-graders then carried the materials into five second-grade classes and passed along what they had learned to the younger students. Jim reported that his students were "amazed by their own success" in grasping the complicated material—and thrilled by the opportunity to take the fossils home, where they became cherished objects. We heard from his students, too. A sixth-grader named Rebecca wrote to us about her experience teaching the second-graders. "When I walked through the door of the classroom," she admitted, "I was real nervous. When I saw all those anxious little second-graders waiting for us to teach something new, I felt more relaxed. I showed them the fossils and their eyes brightened! They all were like, 'Wow!' All the kids were asking lots of smart questions and were real interested. I feel like I made a difference."

When we told our donor about the results of the immediate response grants, he renewed his pledge and added more funds. Other donors joined him, and the effort has continued to grow. But it has never grown out of hand. The efficiency of contact, review, funding, and reporting makes it possible for our modest staff of four to complete all the work.

To date, PVF has given out some $3.5 million in immediate response grants to teachers, social workers, and other professionals working directly with young people—particularly in poor communities.

Seven Steps towards Paperless Giving

MOST GRANTMAKING programs can dramatically reduce the time devoted to the proposal cycle and move closer to the ideal of paperless giving. Over the years at PVF, we've found the following steps helpful.

1. **Spend less time on proposals that will be denied.** Eighty-five percent of proposals get turned down. Don't make them the center of your work. Ask for every proposal to include an abstract as the first page. The abstract can immediately alert you to a request that is ineligible due to location, cause, program design, or size of request—and therefore save you the time of wading through many pages before making the same conclusion.

2. **Triage submissions.** Create a "not favored" status for inadequate proposals so staff can quickly execute the inevitable turndown. Train a volunteer or staff member to pare back your slush pile at least weekly. Only then pass along the contenders to the person with authority to pursue them.

3. **Eliminate duplication.** Ask for a single copy of a proposal. One copy saves room, time, and bother in storing. If you need extra copies, make them yourself.

4. **Pick up the phone and encourage e-mail applications.** Field phone calls from prospective applicants. Ask them to briefly describe their projects, and then tell them if the effort is eligible for consideration. You'll avoid further

action on proposals destined to be denied from the start. Make certain that the staff fielding the calls are experienced, honest, modest, firm, and to the point. Also, try experimenting with grant applications submitted by e-mail. You'll probably find yourself responding quickly, and you'll certainly whittle away at your stack of paper.

5. **Reduce application requirements.** One-page letters of intent can cover three topics: the identity of the applicant; their mission; and a brief summary of the project. That's all you need. For full proposals demand only what will enable you to make a decision—with a limit set at seven to ten pages. The audit, five-year plan, and other documents can come later, if at all.

6. **Professionalize your files.** Filing systems expand over time—and seldom in the direction of order and simplicity. Hire a reference librarian to design a system suited to your needs; they're experts at organizing and delivering materials with speed and accuracy. Or talk with staff at other foundations about the systems that have proven to work for them. Purge your old records ruthlessly. Rejected proposals can be tossed annually. Don't save them.

7. **Enshrine speed and simplicity as the watchwords of your foundation.** Alter your organizational attitude about time. Rely less on paper and put more of your (crucial) information on computer. (Then back it up regularly.) Respect, review, and reward these behaviors with the staff and board.

Minimal Paperwork for Handling Requests

I'LL BE HONEST. Even "paperless giving" requires *some* paper. But it comes nowhere close to conventional grantmaking. In response to the weekly stream of correspondence and requests, our staff takes the following steps:

1. **Situation:** We receive a request outside our geographic region and it's therefore ineligible for consideration.

   Response: Upon receipt, we immediately dispatch a post-card printed with this message:

   > *Dear Friend,*
   >
   > *We have received your request. Please be advised that Philanthropic Ventures Foundation directs the vast major-ity of its funding to activities in the San Francisco Bay Area. Consequently, we cannot be of assistance to you.*

2. **Situation:** We review a proposal that proves too weak to warrant consideration.

   Response: We immediately send a single-page letter stating:

   > *Thank you for your proposal. We're sorry to inform you that it does not meet our present requirements for consideration.*

   If the grantseeker asks for further feedback, I will respond on the phone in a frank and forthright manner. But in order not to invest any more time in a proposal destined for rejection, I avoid doing a written critique.

3. **Situation:** We receive an interesting proposal that we will consider funding.

   Response: Within a week of receipt, we review all pro-posals and send postcards to potential grantees with the following response:

   > *Dear_____,*
   >
   > *We have received your request for funds, and it is sched-uled for consideration at our next meeting, to be held on _____. We will be in touch with you if we need further information.*

4. **Situation:** We receive an excellent proposal meeting our eligibility requirements and requesting a modest sum.

Response: We fund these proposals immediately with discretionary funds, sending out the check along with a letter of transmittal.

The letter of transmittal is one of our most useful tools for reducing paperwork and saving time. The letter runs only one page. It outlines the purpose and terms of the grant. The grantee signs the letter as a receipt and agreement to the terms of the grant, and then faxes a copy to our office. Thus, our initial contact—and contract—are complete.

Time Is Money

BY PARING BACK the procedures and materials related to proposal submission—by far, the bulk of foundation paperwork—it's possible to save an enormous amount of time. But paperwork reduction also saves money. All the dimes and quarters accrued over the course of the year really do add up. Consider the costs of mailing a single letter:

- Envelope: 23¢
- Two sheets of paper, including letterhead: 20¢
- Postage: 41¢—and rising…
- Secretarial labor (15 minutes @ $14/hr): $3.50
- Composing the letter (10 minutes @ $30/hour): $5.00
- Overhead (rent, utilities, equipment): 7¢
- Total: $9.41 per letter

If you reduce your volume of mail by one hundred letters annually, you've just saved $941—enough to outfit your local day care center with a fully loaded desktop computer, send a start-up non-profit's new development director to a week's training session, or pay for a child's tuition at a summer music camp.

But that's only the start. Some foundations employ one or more clerical hands whose duties focus primarily on responding to proposals that have been thoroughly reviewed (and for the most part, rejected) by program officers. It makes no sense to dedicate so much of a foundation's limited resources to a roundabout of clerical tasks producing no social benefit. Paperwork reduction helps put everybody back on the track of productive philanthropy.

Grantmaking on the Run

OCCASIONALLY, I'll encounter grantmaking opportunities out in the field, and we'll dispense altogether with the proposal review process, along with the bureaucratic baggage customarily attached. In a nutshell, this is what happens:

I meet a creative person running an interesting project. He pitches an idea for improving or expanding an important service to the community. We discuss its prospects and determine what's needed to make it work, and then we devise a rough budget on the spot. When I return to my office, I'll write a check and put it in the mail.

But that's not how the foundation world works!

No, it's certainly not. And it isn't the way we make most of our grants at PVF, either. But when everything comes together—the visionary leader, the healthy organization, the promising idea— then I'll set aside the usual procedures and I'll take the necessary risk to set the effort in motion.

Instead of the proposal, letter of interest, staff evaluation, board docket, board decision summary, letter of award, and contract, I use a single paper tool: our trusty letter of transmittal.

I describe in a paragraph the project and goal we have discussed, and I specify the amount awarded. At the bottom of the letter, I leave room for the signature of the person in charge. Once signed, the letter is faxed back to our office. And that's our contract.

But what about the risks, the absence of safeguards and account-ability?

- I take risks. That's part of my job as a philanthropist.

- The only way to protect yourself against your own gross errors in judgment is to know your community, its issues, organizations, and its players. Anything less is merely a tissue of false confidence.

- As far as accountability goes, I demand a great deal more from our nonprofit collaborators—and our foundation— than any five pounds of formal grant reports can provide. I'm concerned about accountability, and that's why I make it a point to visit the projects we fund on multiple occa-sions and often over the course of years. I view grantmak-ing as a relationship. It's up to me to support my end of the relationship with persistent contact, conversation, and physical presence. I'm not interested in a long-distance relationship conducted by mail or computer. To my mind, that's where the real risk—and recklessness—occur.

Trustees with Time to Kill

TOO OFTEN foundation boards add their own layers of bureau-cracy to philanthropy. Instead of relying on staff, they burrow into assignments that prove unnecessary and repetitive. They demand excessive documentation on potential grantees—thereby assuming the appearance of oversight, if not its reality. And they elaborate the duties of governance in ways that only undermine the executive's role and scatter even more paper along the path of grantmaking.

Yet most grievous time-wasting errors can be avoided.

Throughout thirty years in philanthropy, I've watched hundreds of foundation boards strive to effectively dispatch their duties. Most of the time, they chug along bravely without models or training, reinventing themselves every few years as opportunity and necessity may dictate. Given that trustees are usually intelligent and successful people well versed in the organizational cultures of their own professions, they often get their boards operating with a semblance of efficiency, if not dazzling speed or imagination. Yet just as frequently, I see the efforts of shrewd and experienced trustees impeded by the following time-wasting obstacles:

Absence and tardiness: Members miss board and committee meetings, or arrive late and require staff and trustees to bring them up to speed.

Micromanagement: Board members insist on reviewing prospective grants in exhaustive detail, even after the committee charged with this duty has submitted its considered recommendations.

Factionalism: Individuals pursue their own personal agendas in awarding grants—breeding antagonisms among other members, ensuring power struggles, and eventually rending the board into warring factions.

Sometimes these problems lead back to a trustee or two who must be (gently) disciplined by the board chair. If a trustee proves persistently disruptive and unwilling to change his ways, he should be removed—a more complicated matter. On foundation boards, as elsewhere, regime change is always a messy affair, the option of last resort. But a dysfunctional board cannot be allowed to waste the time, financial resources, and moral capital of the foundation. If the board proves inept, inert, or locked in perpetual internecine strife, then changes must occur—most likely with the aid of an outside expert who can redirect the trustees towards their proper role and reform the governance structure. Short of this worst-case scenario, many of a typical board's time-wasting proclivities can be addressed by concentrating on three basic areas:

Schedule: Keep board meetings to a minimum. If the executive is effective, the board can easily dispatch its duties with quarterly meetings—or at most, every other month.

Structure: Most boards only need three standing committees: audit, investment (and development for community foundations), and grants review. The committees should remain small—five members is ideal. If the board itself is small, it might take on responsibility as a whole for all these duties.

Authority: The foundation executive should be the conduit for all information related to grantmaking. Trustees should avoid dealing directly with prospective grantees. Nor should they undertake management tasks, such as approving the payment of bills, personnel, or other decisions better left to the executive.

The Executive Director: the Board's Ultimate Time Saver

THE TRUSTEES' most important duty is to hire (and in less happy circumstances, fire) the executive director. Once they find a good manager, they need to step out of the way and let her run the place.

That's the way the corporate world works, it's what nonprofit organizations strive for, and it's the policy foundations need to adopt if they're to remain nimble and capable of responding to community needs and opportunities. On the executive's part, it's essential to keep the board apprised of the foundation's activities and the rationale linking approved grants to the foundation's mission. In essence, the relationship between executive and board is collaborative. A good board meeting is by definition a celebration of the work accomplished by staff that fulfills the vision articulated by the board.

Of course, the law holds boards responsible for the grants their foundations make—just as corporate and nonprofit boards remain ultimately responsible for their organizations' actions. But responsibility for grants shouldn't be confused with their execution. Boards can delegate a great deal of authority to staff in making decisions and disbursing funds. The situation is analogous to building a house. To design the structure, you engage an architect—the person with vision and skills to create the overall plan. To execute the work, you rely on a general contractor, who in turn hires laborers, plumbers, electricians. In the foundation world, the board is the architect, the executive is the contractor, and any other staff or consultants are the building crew. Board members have no business trying to excavate the basement or fiddling around with the plumbing. And yet, too often, that's exactly what happens.

If a foundation is to run effectively, the executive must be empowered to make executive decisions. These decisions naturally cover the management of daily activities. Anything less is a recipe for organizational paralysis. Less appreciated—and far less frequently embraced—is the recognition that executives should also exercise the lion's share of responsibility for awarding grants.

Of course, a scale of corresponding size and authority inevitably comes into play. In a healthy foundation equipped with a skilled staff and lubricated by trust and the steady flow of information between the executive and trustees, those grants deemed "small"—be they $5,000 or $50,000—can be efficiently handled by the executive director. Small grants usually require a quick response; they can't linger for the convening of the board or its grant committee. (Larger grants requiring board approval can be reviewed by the grants committee, and its recommendations forwarded to the full board.) If board members find they don't trust their executive to make funding decisions, only two options remain: a) resign from the board; or b) fire the executive and find one who does inspire trust.

Numerous advantages accrue to the foundation that gives its executive the authority to approve a significant portion of its grants.

- Grants can be made at the moment of optimum effect: when the money is needed, and not at the arbitrary date of the board's next meeting.

- All the paperwork involved with the review of grants is dramatically reduced.

- The habit of timely grantmaking alters the foundation's organizational culture, making speed and dexterity in decision-making a prime value.

- The foundation's reputation for responsiveness and decisive action quickly spreads throughout the nonprofit and foundation worlds.

- The executive has even more reason and opportunity to take initiative in seeking out worthy projects and outstanding people.

- The entire staff has more time to get out of the office and into the field—and to investigate funding possibilities.

- The board has more time, reason, and enthusiasm to participate in site visits to evaluate grants, and undertake the analysis of grantmaking in relation to the foundation's mission—tasks that add to the foundation's knowledge of the community.

At PVF, we also empower our staff to make grants. I think that's an arrangement worth experimenting with—particularly if you have program officers with designated areas of expertise.

The Right Amount at the Right Time

SPEED IS A VIRTUE in grantmaking. But on the scale of virtues, timeliness ranks even higher.

By timeliness, I mean the art of delivering precisely the right amount of money at precisely the right moment to have the optimum impact. In other words, speed combines with accuracy to trump size. In fact, the best-timed grants usually don't involve a great deal of money.

I'll give you a couple of examples.

A few years ago, I received a phone call from a juvenile court judge requesting a small grant to assist a thirteen-year-old boy. He was named Josh, and he'd been recently removed from his mother's care when she became homeless and began living in her car. Josh entered a group home, fared badly with the separation from his mom, and seemed to be withdrawing painfully into himself without the care and affection he needed. The judge was a very perceptive man, and he recognized an unusual opportunity to help this boy. Josh was a great animal lover, and he lived near the Redwing Horse Sanctuary, a place that cared for abused and neglected animals. For a small sum, Josh could "adopt" Niner, one of the Sanctuary's donkeys, and visit him on weekly trips with his mother.

The grant for the adoption fee totaled forty dollars.

The only hitch was that the judge needed it immediately.

I wrote the check and sent it out in the afternoon mail.

A few weeks later, I heard back from the judge, who passed along a message from the district attorney. The D.A. reported that the weekly visits to Niner at the Sanctuary were "the one thing that kept Josh going."

A preposterously small sum delivered at the right moment made all the difference.

In truth, these kinds of opportunities avail themselves quite frequently to foundations that have the capacity to respond quickly.

Last year, we learned from one of our grantees about a young single mother with five children who was about to lose her mobile home in East Palo Alto because of her ex-husband's outstanding debts. Defaulting on the mortgage would have proved catastrophic for the family and costly for the county. The family's chief asset, their home equity—the rock that many working families use to pull themselves into the middle class—would have melted away. And the children would have been placed in custodial care, perhaps for years, all at the taxpayers' expense. Through the East Palo Alto Community Law Project, our foundation made a $5,000 grant the mother requested to prevent foreclosure. She raised another $9,000 through "prayers, working overtime, and salary advances" from her two jobs with office-cleaning companies. "Since I was so lucky to get the $5,000 from PVF, I had to do my share," she told us. "I just had to." She and her five children were saved from homelessness, and they now own the mobile home.

When Speed Saves Lives: Disaster Relief

FOLLOWING Hurricane Katrina in 2005, I visited Louisiana and Mississippi to see what PVF could do to help.

My first stop was Memphis, where many national and regional philanthropies had gathered to discuss the catastrophe. Then I moved on to Baton Rouge to talk with folks working at several local foundations.

Everybody was facing the same problem. Government agencies, individual donors, and private foundations all wanted to help, but what they could accomplish was gravely limited by their lack of familiarity with local leaders and nonprofit agencies that could be depended on in a crisis. Sure, they knew all the usual players, the people they had funded over the years through the conventional process of proposal submission and approval. But that kind of grantmaking was unthinkable in Katrina's wake. Besides, how do you consult the people charged with rebuilding after the hurricane when you can't find them? How do you work with nonprofit agencies when they don't know where their employees are? How do you even know what's happening in the most severely stricken areas when the roads have been engulfed by toxic pools, telecommunications have collapsed, and most employees in the human service sector have fled town?

Believe me, as a lifetime resident of the San Francisco Bay Area, I've thought long and hard about natural disasters. The Bay Area is earthquake country. We all know that someday we will be hit by a huge quake whose destructiveness may equal or even exceed the devastation wrought by Katrina.

In preparation, we've done some planning at PVF that I think makes sense in every community—whether it contends with the looming threat of earthquake, hurricane, flood, tornado, or some unseen and unpredictable peril.

At PVF, we have identified ten outstanding organizations whose operations we've funded over the years. Each group has a long track record of working directly with the poor—providing housing, health care, and education. Their leaders and staff are rooted in the community, committed for the long haul.

We've signed a letter of understanding with each organization, stating that in the event of a major earthquake, fire, flood, or other disaster, they have immediate access to twenty-five thousand dollars for the first four days following the event. The organizations' leaders may use their personal credit cards for any charges they deem necessary in alleviating harm and suffering, with the knowledge that they will be reimbursed by PVF before the charges fall due. We don't tell them what to do with the money; they don't need to check with us before spending it. We trust these folks to make decisions on the ground and in the midst of chaos. We trust them to do so because we know their work, their organizations, and the character of the people involved.

In this way, we've placed one quarter of a million dollars into play in the first hour of disaster. And we've also encouraged our nonprofit partners, along with our own staff and board, to prepare today for the crises that will occur someday, without fail, though none of us can say when.

Timeliness Pays Off

OVER THE YEARS, I've worked hard to speed up our grantmaking and free it from the paper shackles of bureaucracy. My motivation has been pragmatic: too much good work remains to be done in philanthropy for us to waste any time.

I've also discovered a pleasing dividend in our efforts to quicken the pace of philanthropy.

It turns out that the people who contribute to PVF also like to save time, pass on the paperwork, and skip past the bureaucracy. They enjoy seeing their money spent quickly, wisely, and to demonstrable effect.

In some community foundations, donors establish funds and then sit on them for years, waiting for some ideal moment to make their grants. We discourage this kind of behavior at PVF. We show donors why today (or at least, tomorrow) is the right time to take their first philanthropic steps. And when donors see the impact of timely giving, they grow enthusiastic about the possibilities of philanthropy and they give even more generously.

It's a case of everybody winning—sooner, rather than later.

6 The Joys of Risk

Principle #3:
Embrace risk

"Chance favors the trained mind."
—*Louis Pasteur*

PHILANTHROPY THRIVES on risk.

It is risk that fuels our grantmaking engines, pushes us uphill, leads us in new directions.

And yet risk also terrifies most foundation executives and boards.

That's because one possible outcome of risk-taking is failure. And far more than most powerful institutions—certainly more than the corporate sector or government—foundations dread the prospect of acknowledging their shortcomings and mistakes.

That's why foundation grantmaking tends to be timid, predictable, and far less productive than it could be.

It's one of the ironies of organized philanthropy that for all our talk about transforming the world, most foundation directors and trustees pride themselves on their balance, sobriety, stability—the sort of institutional values that comport with Hollywood notions of a stiff-necked, starch-collared banker. In truth, bankers take far more risks than foundation executives. They must—otherwise, they could never make a living.

Foundations don't have to make a living. They're endowed. And the safety net provided by our endowments paradoxically encourages us to play it safer than we need. In the end, we squander our natural advantages—our immense wealth, our autonomy, our ability to swim against the tide of public opinion and social convention when they undermine justice, progress, and possibility.

Please understand, I am not advocating risk for its own sake, nor do I flatter myself as being a kind of philanthropic daredevil. And I certainly don't equate risk-taking with gambling. Gambling relies on fate, happenstance, the teeth-clenched, long-odds possibility of a satisfactory outcome. I consider gambling in philanthropy to be just another word for throwing your money into the street and hoping the winds of chance will somehow carry it to a better place. Gambling inevitably ends with losses we can't afford.

When grantmakers embrace risk, it's because they perceive an opportunity to make changes that would otherwise prove impossible. Risk-taking in philanthropy is chiefly a matter of summoning the courage to question the old ways and try something new.

Putting the Venture Back into "Venture Philanthropy"

IN RECENT YEARS, many foundation executives have extolled the virtues of "venture philanthropy." They've culled the term from "venture capitalism"—the strategy of high-risk investments undertaken in profuse numbers with the aim of eventually yielding huge profits. In place of the investor's conventional ROI, or return on investment, philanthropists seek a SROI (social return on investment), ROH (return on humanity), or ROC (return on community)—all rather oblique ways of saying "the result we were aiming for."

The problem with this analogy is that the venture capitalist's ROI is nothing at all like SROI, ROH, ROC, or any other term you care to use to indicate social progress. In the venture capital model, investors desire one thing only: profit, the more the better. In its pursuit, they sacrifice a vast amount of money to many, many doomed ventures in hopes of securing a single enormous success that will wildly compensate for the losses.

That's not how philanthropy works.

Our grant portfolios are diverse not because we're tracking down one great redeeming score. Rather, we fund various projects in numerous fields because the work that needs doing in our communities—day care, education, community organizing, and the like—is varied, disparate, and dispersed. Every effort we support must succeed or fail on its own terms. A brilliant success in day care, for example, can't compensate for a long line of unproductive grants in education.

Other differences between venture capitalism and venture philanthropy abound. Nevertheless, foundation professionals can still derive a valuable lesson from the exploits of venture capitalists.

To state this lesson plainly: Nothing ventured, nothing gained… To achieve great things, grantmakers must take commensurate risks.

I should state right now that "venture philanthropy" is a term I have been using for more than twenty years. But whenever I speak to my peers about venture philanthropy, I am not suggesting that we tear a page out of corporate America's play book—or even that we adopt such commonsense business practices as establishing clear performance measures, making grants over longer time horizons, or devoting far more resources to strengthening organizational capacity. What I'm really talking about is grantmaking characterized by:

- Creative ideas
- Potential for high-yield impact
- Thorough research and abiding relationships

I realize that most foundation directors would insist that they already frame their grants with these goals precisely in mind. Personally, I think the record indicates otherwise, but for the moment I'll set aside my objections. Instead, let me try to express the essence of what I believe to be genuine venture philanthropy in a single word: *Trust*.

Trust is the indispensable factor in making philanthropic risk acceptable. It's what provides balance and confidence when the outcome looms uncertainly. Trust allows us to strike out for the roads unexplored by our grantmaking brethren.

Where does trust come from? Experience.

Experience with the applicant organization that ensures a deep knowledge of its aims and accomplishments. Experience with the director, her work history, and her previous achievements. Experience in the field that gives the grantmaker a thorough understanding of the project's potential impact and probable obstacles.

And how does one gather experience?

At this point, you should not be astonished to hear that I believe it depends almost entirely on one crucial action: getting out of your office and into the field.

The main reason philanthropists prove so timid in their grantmaking is that they lack the basis for wisely calculating risk. They fail to cultivate deep, varied, and continuing experience in the field. And without experience, even the best-intended efforts, even the most openhearted and courageous risk-taking, will end up looking like naiveté or even foolhardiness.

Trust derived of formative *experience* with *outstanding nonprofit leaders*: these are the irreducible elements of venture philanthropy in its most vital and creative guise.

Risks I'm Glad I've Taken

I KNOW WHEN I'm taking a risk. I feel slightly on edge, a bit uneasy. I'm aware that I have made a decision to support an unproven project, and as a result, our foundation could fall flat on its face. It's not a feeling I relish. But I realize it comes with the territory.

I also know when I'm not taking enough risks. I feel *too* comfortable. Uncertainty doesn't rattle my bones at odd moments in the night. I'm satisfied that our grantmaking is spinning along with unruffled predictability. I sleep better than I deserve.

That's when I know it's time to stick my neck out—even though I could play turtle and hide in the hard shell of philanthropic convention.

What does risk-taking look like at Philanthropic Ventures Foundation (PVF)? Here are three grants we made that most foundations wouldn't have touched:

- The editor of a local newspaper introduced me to a free-lance Latina journalist who quickly directed PVF to several outstanding nonprofit directors serving the immigrant population. One month after our first meeting, PVF awarded the journalist a ten-thousand-dollar grant to be used at her discretion to benefit Oakland's Spanish-speaking community. The funds ended up supporting a variety of small but important funding opportunities that PVF would not have otherwise known about: bonus incentives for community workers within a struggling nonprofit that provided key services to the low-income community; a field trip for a youth leadership group; emergency aid for two undocumented immigrants who had become victims of street crime; a retreat for Spanish-speaking mothers who were creating a support circle within their local elementary school; and a Spanish-language training program to introduce nonprofits to local grantmakers—a program now offered regularly by our local Foundation Center.

  As with most funds dedicated to discretionary use, this grant proved risky from the start—all the more so because our relationship with the grantee was so new.

- PVF made two grants of seventeen thousand dollars to cover the salaries of two Latina mothers charged with helping Spanish-speaking parents understand the challenges their children faced in school and encouraging them to attend parent/teacher meetings and become more active in their children's education. Both women were recent graduates of an ESL program, but otherwise had minimal education and no formal training for their positions. Indeed, without PVF funding, their respective school principals would never have taken the chance of hiring them. Yet over time, the benefits accrued to the students, families, classroom teachers, and the two women have proved enormous. Taking this risk also pointed PVF in a useful new direction: to date, we have made grants in excess of one hundred thousand dollars to underwrite the costs of grassroots parental outreach workers.

- A Stanford undergraduate developed an unusually effective program for encouraging young people in foster care to pursue higher education—an issue of particular interest to the student, who had once been in foster care himself. Working with young trainers, the Stanford student showed social workers and child advocates how to encourage foster youth to attend college, secure financial aid, and connect with reliable mentors. PVF awarded a grant of five thousand dollars to develop an online component of the program. The program's founder soon graduated from Stanford, leaving the online project in new hands. Today he continues to do outstanding advocacy work with foster youth. But without its "Sparker," the online component soon lost steam and collapsed; the risk we took with this part of the project simply didn't pay off.

As you can see, two out of three of these risky grants succeeded—which may be as good as anyone can reasonably expect. (If you're batting 100 percent in your grantmaking, you're either not looking closely enough at the results or you're taking too few risks.)

What led PVF to assume the risks embedded in these three grants?

- I knew the community and the problems people routinely faced there.
- I trusted the people recommending support.
- I met with the individuals directly involved with the projects prior to funding them, and I had a good feeling about each one.

In other words, I relied on both my head and my heart.

That's right—my gut feelings, my intuition, played a key role in approving each grant.

Over the years, I've come to think of intuition as an indispensable tool for grantmakers, an internal compass fine-tuned with the recollection of past experience that allows us to make important decisions within milliseconds. Intuition is the voice that emerges from a lifetime of learning and tells us yes or no—long before we can state precisely why.

Trusting our intuition can prove challenging. To other people, the highly intuitive grantmaker can look like the unconscious agent of reckless snap judgments. Somebody easily duped. A fool. At the very least, we may appear *unreasonable* to our peers, and that's not a word most of us care to see pinned to our reputations. More often, it's our own self-doubt that throws the brakes on intuition. The sudden, spooky arrival of the voice within can frighten us. "*Where did that come from?*" we wonder—and there's really no satisfying answer.

At PVF, our openness to intuition enables us to take venture philanthropy one step further. Like all thoughtful grantmakers, we fund projects based on sound organizations and exciting ideas. But we also support and sometimes even instigate activity because of the bedrock confidence we place in a project's leaders. It all comes back to my first principle in grantmaking: find outstanding people—people you can trust—and fund them.

Sometimes, my experience with the leader is limited. Occasionally, I'll make a decision within days or even hours of meeting somebody impressive. I've even funded folks on the spot—astonishing them, and sometimes myself as well.

We ignore our intuition at our own peril. If we insist on waiting for all the evidence to line up in support of a grant with the clarity of a geometric proof, then we're going to get stuck. Without well-founded trust in our own instincts, we lapse into paralysis.

Grants to Individuals

I FREQUENTLY HEAR from other foundation officers and trustees that PVF's grantmaking to individuals represents a breach in federal regulations and poses a grave risk of censure from the IRS. Foundations, they explain with inevitable pique and impatience, cannot make grants to individuals.

They're wrong.

Federal law states that grants must be used exclusively for charitable purposes. Over the years, the concept of charitable purpose has melded with and morphed into the 501(c)(3) tax-exempt nonprofit organization. In the eyes of most foundations, they're synonymous.

Yet charitable purpose and charitable organizations are not one and the same. Individuals engaged in charitable work can also qualify for foundation support. It's just that foundations find it simpler, less risky, and most of all, less demanding, to reject out of hand the appeals of individuals. In a sense, grantmakers cede their own judgment to the IRS in regard to what constitutes charitable purpose. Ironically, the IRS demonstrates little enthusiasm for playing this role.

Concern about the IRS is the apparent cause for most foundations' dismissal of individual grants. The more important, unacknowledged factor is that foundation staff usually aren't sufficiently acquainted with their communities to identify the outstanding individuals who deserve support.

Anybody can respond to finely crafted proposals from well-positioned organizations. Only a foundation vested in the community can locate, identify, and establish partnerships with the leading individual activists.

Let's face the truth. If you choose not to make grants to artists, ad hoc groups of mothers offering after-school recreation, or fledgling organizations that have yet to obtain nonprofit status, this decision is your own—not one imposed by the IRS.

Of course, it's conceivable that at some point your grants might be challenged by the IRS, and you will need to prove that the individual grantee's work truly provides public benefit. How can you know if your money achieves its intended philanthropic intent? By dismantling the conventional foundation bureaucracy and undertaking the real work of accountability: thorough, continuing, frank, and honest contact with the people you fund. It's illusory to think that the paper handcuffs shackling most nonprofits—the bulky applications, support materials, and periodic reports—will constrain incompetence or criminality. Your only real protection is to know the people you fund.

Consider these three small grants we made to individuals:

- A social worker called me about a sixteen-year-old girl in foster care who had located a part-time job and enrolled in summer school. But she didn't have money for transportation. PVF passed the money along to pay for her bus pass.

- A clergyman told me about a young mother and daughter who had recently moved to a shelter for battered women after being harassed by the ex-husband, who had just been released after being convicted and jailed for spousal abuse. Both mother and child feared leaving the shelter, even for a few hours. We paid to activate an emergency cell phone that kept them in contact and provided a link to the police.

- A sculptor approached us for support on a public art project. We paid him a stipend for the time required to complete the installation.

All three grants were dependent on personal recommendations from outside our staff. Nonprofit agencies helped in their application, oversight, and evaluation.

How did our risk-taking with individuals turn out?

The teenage girl finished her summer courses, kept her job, and went on to graduate from high school. The mother and daughter remained safe, soon relocated to another community, and started their lives over in an environment free from violence and intimidation. And the sculptor—well…he never finished his project. I made inquiries, but soon after, he vanished from town. Of the three grantees, he had appeared from the start to be the best bet, equipped with a long track record of artistic acclaim and group and individual exhibitions.

But he took the money and ran—the worst possible outcome.

It happens. Not often, but every once in a while, one of our riskier ventures with individuals will unravel into undeniable failure. It's better to face this hard truth from the start and not let it blindside you—or worse, let it prevent you from acting.

Of course, I did learn something valuable from our experience with the disappearing sculptor. The next time I fund a public art project—and there *will* be a next time—I'll establish a clearer set of benchmarks, meting out funds in small amounts, and thereby helping the artist pass through the inevitable frustrations of creation with the lure of the next payment.

It will still be a risk.

But risk is something foundations are uniquely equipped to undertake. I believe it's irresponsible to do otherwise. If foundations can't take risks, nobody can.

Very High Trust: Discretionary Grants

OVER THE YEARS, PVF has experimented with an unusual kind of risk-taking in the form of discretionary grants. We search for committed people working in strategic positions of public service—the schools, courts, probation departments, and mental health agencies—and we hand over to them the responsibility and the funds to make numerous small grants over the course of a year to meet the emergency needs of the people they serve.

Our partners in this enterprise know firsthand about the inequities and injustices that afflict our society. As a result, they invariably come up with creative, practical ideas for addressing them. While serving as our eyes and ears in the most troubled corners of the community, they use their own judgment about how to spend their grant allocations. There's no application, review process, or lag time. It's high-trust philanthropy, grounded in a continuing relationship with the people who work each day at the most intimate levels of human suffering, need, and service.

Here's how the practice evolved.

Ten years ago, I spent some time interviewing juvenile court judges in the Bay Area. I wanted to learn what the judges viewed as the determinant forces shaping, and too often shattering, the lives of the vulnerable young people who came before the bench. The judges told me that the children and teenagers they saw carried the burden of a vast assortment of crucial, but relatively inexpensive, needs. They had seen countless children fail to flourish for want of a pair of eyeglasses, dental work, psychotherapy; sometimes just a new pair of shoes that allowed a child to attend school without shame. But no mechanism existed to place these items or services at their disposal.

PVF allocated ten thousand dollars each to juvenile court judges in Santa Clara and San Mateo Counties, with the understanding that they would identify and then take steps to meet the needs of the kids passing through their courtrooms. The judges arranged for services to be rendered and purchases to be made, with the bills sent directly to our foundation. Within a few weeks, we received brief reports about how the discretionary funds were being spent.

- $100 to start a savings account for a teenager struggling with mental illness who had recently "graduated" from juvenile court to an adult mental health program. The judge wanted this gesture "to help confirm in the young man's mind that there are people in the world who care and who keep their promises."

- $200 for summer science camp benefiting a young girl in foster care whose sudden enthusiasm for biology had caused her to refocus her efforts on school and curtail her self-destructive behavior.

- $600 for a young woman leaving a state youth prison, to pay for tuition and a uniform to attend trade school.

With time, the discretionary grants grew more imaginative—though not necessarily more costly. One judge helped teen mothers who had no previous experience with banking to open savings accounts for their children. (PVF made the first $100 deposit.) Other grants underwrote: the court costs for a juvenile's legal name change; the printing of posters about community resources countering domestic violence; a luncheon bringing youth together with police officers; summer camp for many children who had never before journeyed outside their own inner-city neighborhoods; travel costs to unite siblings for the holidays; uniforms, school clothes, books, musical instruments, and bicycles; or just a small gift certificate to acknowledge a significant accomplishment such as full attendance at school and improved grades. In short, these discretionary grants underwrote everything that middle-class children normally take for granted—but that had been neglected amid the chaos of these kids' troubled upbringing.

The grants also sparked interest from other professionals, who saw how far a small amount of money could go. A deputy district attorney with Santa Clara County contacted PVF on behalf of her client—a fifteen-year-old who had been severely physically abused by his father and bounced back and forth between foster homes and family placements. The deputy D.A. went on to explain that the boy was "deeply depressed, won't go to school because he is so far behind, and he won't eat and can't sleep. One thing, however, sparks his interest: any kind of art." The court opted to purchase art supplies and enroll him in an art class "to help build his self-esteem, give him some stability, and improve his outlook on life." For less than two hundred dollars, PVF helped a conscientious deputy D.A. lift this boy out of his immobilizing depression and onto a more hopeful and positive path.

In San Mateo County, the Juvenile Drug Court tried another strategy, handing out ten-dollar gift certificates for Target, The Wherehouse, and Tower Records as positive reinforcement for drug-free behavior. Ten dollars may seem insignificant to most adults. But for children without resources or parental support, the certificates not only provided an opportunity to purchase a much coveted item; their formal presentation by the judge also served as a symbol of progress in their struggle towards sobriety.

One unanticipated outcome of the discretionary grant program has been to bolster morale among people working within a justice system fiercely bound by financial constraints. "The grants have made my job as a juvenile court judge much more satisfying," Judge Leonard Edwards of Santa Clara County Superior Court told us. "The support that PVF provides on an individualized basis for the abused and neglected children in my court brightens my day and makes the lives of these children much more livable."

Care and Feeding of Discretionary Grant Programs

WHEN A NEW police chief took charge in East Palo Alto, one of the Bay Area's most troubled communities, I sent him a letter committing PVF to a ten-thousand-dollar grant to be used at his discretion. The chief immediately phoned our office. He was pleased, but puzzled. Where was the hitch, the gimmick, the hidden agenda? He'd never heard of a foundation engaging in such a practice. He and I got together for lunch, and I explained how the discretionary grants had fared with the juvenile court judges. Soon we had an understanding, and the beginnings of a fruitful partnership.

I understand why the police chief initially felt suspicious about our overture. Discretionary grants do seem too good to be true. But that's only because we've grown accustomed to the narrow dimensions of foundation giving. In reality, discretionary grants rank as just another neglected tool that philanthropy could routinely use to address community needs that otherwise rate as too small or idiosyncratic for the conventional grant application process. Any foundation can launch a discretionary grant program. Yet few choose to do so. Why? For many, a lack of knowledge about their communities limits possibilities. For others, the discretionary grant is simply an option that just hasn't occurred to them, and hasn't been modeled by other funders.

At PVF, we know that the only way to continue our discretionary grantmaking is to maintain our commitment to getting out into the field, where we can make contact with remarkable people undertaking important work. No study, book, conference, consultant, or professional gathering can substitute for a lack of pavement pounding. We can assume the risks inherent in discretionary grants because we have confidence in our knowledge of the community.

But it takes more than continuing research and trustworthy partners. Foundations also must consciously set aside the money to use for discretionary grants. Most foundations commit their funds to established categories, with the staff enjoying limited flexibility in redirecting grants to meet sudden opportunities.

That's why I now routinely ask that funders allocate a portion of their gifts to PVF to our unrestricted funds. I explain how the money gets used in poor communities, often reshaping an individual's life for an absurdly small sum. The human stories behind these grants intrigue experienced philanthropists and frequently result in even more generous giving. And by simply broaching the topic with donors, we're both reminded: every success was a risk when it started.

There's one other reason why I raise the possibility of donors dedicating some portion of their gifts to discretionary grantmaking.

If I don't ask, it won't happen.

To make risk-taking possible in philanthropy, you have to personally take the risk of explaining to your board, staff, and supporters what you intend to do—and ask for their help.

Failure and the Fear Factor

ON THE WALL above my desk, I've pinned a note card reading, "When success is assured, an organization becomes inert. It lacks the ability to become a self-correcting institution."

In other words: We learn from our mistakes.

Yet in philanthropy, we can pretend that we don't make any mistakes—never mind blunder into blatant egg-on-face failures. And thereby, we neglect the painful but necessary task of self-correction.

If you foul up in business and refuse to take corrective measures, you go bankrupt. If you work for somebody else and prove ineffectual at your job, you get fired. Even in government, the persistently bungling politician will eventually find himself voted out of office.

Foundations are different. Year after year, we can make middling, unimaginative grants, budging the world not one iota closer towards being a better place, and yet we don't go out of business, lose our jobs, or sacrifice our positions and power. We don't have to take a long hard look at our mistakes, and nobody can compel us to learn from our failures unless we want to.

In truth, philanthropic efforts frequently fail.

Projects we fund generate meager results. Organizations we've backed for years wither and die. Nonprofit leaders we count on to continue the good fight resign, retire, or seek work in better-paid professions. And the global problems we aim to eradicate—hunger, ignorance, injustice—continue to hurl themselves against our best efforts, their power seemingly unmitigated by our resolve.

But we don't talk about failure.

Isn't knowing what doesn't work as important as knowing what does?

Imagine if foundation staff could consult an annual Big Book of Failure—a compendium of the pitfalls embedded in various grantmaking strategies. Think of the time, energy, and money we would all save if we could become acquainted with the devil residing in the details of our colleagues' best-laid plans.

I'm not suggesting that foundations indulge in some masochistic rite of public handwringing, keening over their errors and promising somehow to do better next year. I'm simply saying that we should act like adults: when failure shows up at our doorsteps, look him straight in the eye; then embrace the lessons he has to offer. Not only will we benefit from advertising the perils of fashionable but unproductive practices; or advance our colleagues' agendas by telling the truth about programs that work well in one place but do not relocate gracefully; or improve our grantmaking judgment. We'll also reinforce the philanthropic sector with a bracing degree of modesty.

Personally, I'd like to see the Council of Foundations cap off its annual meetings with a session dedicated to trumpeting our collective shortcomings. I'm looking forward to the time when individual foundations jazz up their annual reports with a few pages covering "This Year's Three Biggest Mistakes."

Sure, the celebration of failure is a hard sell in American society. We revel in success, regard failure as shameful and loathsome. But I genuinely believe that failure is not so dire an outcome as long as it reflects judicious risk-taking, energy, and courage—coupled with a willingness to learn.

Bill Hewlett, cofounder of Hewlett-Packard, used to tell his engineers that if they didn't produce any failures, they weren't doing their jobs right. That's a lesson we should all take to heart.

Controversial Ideas as Risk

ONE OF THE GREATEST services that foundations could render American society would be to wade out into the great sea of critical issues that now threaten to swamp us and take them on without fear of the controversy and opposition they may engender.

Every grantmaker has his own personal list of issues he'd love to tackle—*if only*...I've heard many grantmakers talk about the need to address:

- Universal health care—whose shameful absence is persistently overlooked by both parties in the political process
- The erosion of Constitutional rights—whose neglect threatens the foundation of our democracy
- Poverty, the spawning ground for almost all other social ills—whose eradication currently attracts less than 12 percent of all foundation giving

Not nearly enough grantmaking gets directed towards these hot-button issues; never enough.

I contend that *now* is the moment for philanthropists to launch into innovative grantmaking on these and other issues. After all, what do we have to lose? Philanthropists rank as the most privileged and protected of all professionals. If we can't risk controversy, who can?

Keep in mind that if activists had waited for consensus, there would have never been successful campaigns for universal suffrage, fair labor laws, or civil rights. In each case, courageous philanthropists lent their assistance to the people doing the hard and often dangerous work in the trenches of political reform. The personal risk afforded funders was minimal; their assistance crucial. The potential returns for this kind of risk-taking remain incalculable.

Final Requirement for Risk-taking: Self-Knowledge

WHEN I FEEL something strongly, as I often do, you can read all about it on my face. I'm particularly emotional about philanthropy. Sometimes, I'll find myself choking up in the midst of a public speech about one of our projects.

But that's me—it's neither good nor bad, but simply the way I'm constructed.

The important thing is that I know enough about myself to realize that my emotional responses accompany me into every grantmaking venture. I must consider their effect, or suffer the consequences.

That's particularly true when it comes to taking risks.

If I didn't factor my emotions into each grantmaking equation, I might fail to recognize that my strong feelings sometimes make people uneasy. A sudden demonstration of feeling may scare individuals, cut off communication, inject an element of suspicion into an early alliance. And if I possessed less awareness about my own emotional makeup, I might fall prey to "rescue funding"—tossing a financial line to a charitable ship that's destined to sink no matter what I do.

I don't try to tamp down my feelings or attempt to be somebody else. It's not how I care to live my life. Anyway, I know it would prove futile. I am who I am: virtues, vices, and everything in between. More important, I know who I am.

So let me offer one final rule for philanthropic risk-taking.

Know thyself—so that you can have a clear vision of how to be helpful in changing the rest of the world...That's one of the soundest ways of minimizing, or at least managing, risk.

7 The Trouble with Problems and the Glory of Ideas

Principle #4:

Focus on ideas instead of problems

> *"Our world needs more generosity and it needs more*
> *justice. The challenge is to make the connection so that*
> *everyone sees generosity on the road to justice."*
>
> —*Dave Toycen*, The Power of Generosity

AMERICANS LIKE TO THINK of themselves as problem solvers. It's part of our national mythology—our cult of no-nonsense practicality. We define our work in terms of problems. Problem statements framed by entrepreneurs. Problem sets massaged to resolution by MBA students. Social problems and problems in management and governance discussed endlessly and sometimes even forthrightly engaged by community leaders, politicians, nonprofit organizations, and—yes!—philanthropists.

But seeing the world exclusively in terms of problems proves to be a knotty problem in itself.

To begin, the pervasive emphasis on problems pricks the balloon of energetic idealism, deflating all but the most robust activists. I'm speaking of that worn-to-a-frazzle gloominess that characterizes far too much nonprofit and philanthropic effort. Where's the sense of excitement and possibility, I often wonder, where's the joy? Why would anybody enlist to join our ranks when adversity casts a constant shadow over so many heads?

Then there's the matter of exaggeration.

If the world is truly awash in problems, then your problem had better appear to be the biggest iceberg on the horizon if it's to attract public notice. And what's wrong with a bit of strategic emphasis now and then? Isn't that a useful way to make a point? Ultimately, I believe, it's counterproductive. The need to constantly raise the profile of every problem in a problem-saturated world turns both nonprofits and foundations into boys crying wolf. The tendency towards inflating problems diminishes our power to persuade an increasingly dubious public of the urgency of our issues.

Take homelessness. For decades now, advocates for the homeless have inflated the numbers of the homeless population on our city streets—as though the flesh-and-blood reality weren't bad enough. In addition to exaggerating the size of the homeless population, many advocates echo the war cry *"We're all just a paycheck away from being homeless ourselves!"* But this is patently untrue. Americans may be mired in consumer debt, unable to pay for their children's college, unprepared for their own retirement, and vulnerable to layoffs, jobs shipped overseas, and dwindling pension funds—but that's not the same thing as being a month away from the abject penury and helplessness that characterize life on the street. Worse, this penchant for overstatement covers up the actual roots of chronic homelessness: drug and alcohol addiction and the lack of effective rehabilitation services; the abandonment of mentally ill people in the name of "deinstitutionalization"; the revolving door of incarceration that spits vulnerable people back out into fractured neighborhoods, further brutalized and utterly unprepared to cope; and the reduction of single-resident occupancy units in gentrified urban centers. The "problem" of homelessness turns out to be a multi-headed hydra of complication. In the end, homelessness—like most social "problems"—can't be reduced to a single image or catchphrase; it's textured, nuanced, and contradictory. Exaggeration obscures its true nature and undermines efforts to get a grip on strategies that might produce real change.

Finally, and perhaps most important, I think that philanthropy's orientation towards problems disrupts our timing, fatally. We don't take action until a problem bubbles up into crisis. Instead of being actors in the social order, we become *re*actors, squandering our independence and power. And the problems remain as intractable as ever.

Ideas Instead of Problems

WHAT'S THE ALTERNATIVE?

I believe that, rather than indulging in the rhetoric of a problem-laden universe, we need to emphasize the far richer currency of ideas.

By "idea," I simply mean this: what you want to happen, and how you will bring it about.

Easy to say. Hard, but absolutely necessary, to wrestle with.

Which brings me to Michelangelo.

"Every block of stone has a statue inside it," the great artist once declared, "and it is the task of the sculptor to discover it."

This statement has resonated with me for decades now. I think that's because in grantmaking, there's also a bit of artistry—if we do it right. We stare at the granite blocks of reality, and within them we should perceive not problems, but potentialities. Michelangelo's formula suggests the energy residing in the most inert materials, the possibilities inherent in human vision. As philanthropists, we can attack the stoniest aspects of our social order with all the tools at our disposal, and eventually a vital, creative design will emerge.

I'm arguing that rather than fall back into reaction and the dogged resignation that drags down many efforts, we should assume a creative stance that will elevate grantmaking with a sense of hope and possibility. An emphasis on ideas instead of problems also militates against the nonprofit sector's resistance to change, its reluctance to experiment, and its pandemic burnout. I know that's not the way most folks in the nonprofit and foundation world like to think of themselves, but my experience over three decades tells me it's true. More than most important players in American society, the nonprofit and philanthropic sectors have mired themselves in shopworn tradition, if only because the external forces that might otherwise insist on innovation (say, stockholders or voters) do not exist.

Let me repeat: A problem orientation spurs on *re*action. An *idea* is more powerfully linked to the unfolding process of original thinking, a first step in creating a better world.

I'll give you an example from our experience at Philanthropic Ventures Foundation (PVF).

One day, I was approached by a donor who told me she had been thinking about the plight of poor women—the relentless grind of their daily duties, the absence of small comforts, the sense of guilt, resignation, and despair that made life even more difficult than it need be.

"I think low-income women should have a day off," our donor told me. "Everybody else does."

I'd never quite heard anybody express these sentiments, but to me it made instinctive sense. Our donor wasn't thinking about poor women as a "problem" whose lives could be solved. Rather, she recognized in these women a shared humanity, and it made her wonder what might be done for them to make their days less onerous.

I took this observation as my marching orders and soon we created the Day Off Program.

Let me admit right now that we all knew we'd embarked on a risky endeavor. But rather than worry about a flood of requests that might overwhelm us, or the prospect of being hustled by some unscrupulous applicant, we decided to take the risk, do something nobody else had done before in philanthropy, and see what happened.

I called up school principals, social workers, and members of the clergy we had worked with in the past and asked them to nominate women they knew for a day off. The criteria were simple: we were looking for low-income women who hadn't received a lot of breaks in their lives and could use one now. The nominations immediately rolled in. Once identified, we gave each woman two hundred dollars, through her nominator, with instructions to spend the money on herself to rejuvenate her mind, body, and soul (which frequently met resistance, as many mothers wanted to buy items for their kids). Several women spent the day getting their hair and nails done. One went to the movies alone, gloriously free from the usual demands of the day. Another treated her sister to lunch, and then they spent the afternoon strolling along the ocean shore.

In short, they did the sort of thing middle-class women and men do all the time for themselves.

One participant wrote to us a few days after her day off: "This is the first time anyone has ever given me anything." And I knew we had done something worthwhile.

Did the Day Off Program change the social and economic conditions that keep these women in poverty? No. But for many, it proved a rare experience of appreciation—a recognition that somebody (several somebodies, in fact) understood their lives to be valuable and their struggles deserving of support.

And it all came about in a feat of unbridled imagination—an idea rendered into reality. We could have spent years thinking about the "problem" of poverty and never have landed on such a forthrightly audacious action as this.

Creative Daydreaming and the Call of Ideas

I'VE ALWAYS BEEN a daydreamer. As a child, it got me into trouble. ("Bill," asked my teachers, "just where are you?") In my career as a philanthropist, my propensity for daydreaming—let's call it "creative speculation"—has served me far better. Indeed, I consider it as important a skill as knowing how to read a budget, conduct a meeting, or negotiate a grant.

I believe that moments of repose—daydreaming, if you will—are crucial to creativity. Yet most people in the philanthropic and nonprofit sectors seem too busy to engage in daydreams. (We all know that the overbooked calendar is an unmistakable symbol of prestige...) And that's a shame because incessant busy-ness means key people don't take time to pause, ponder, and then bear down intellectually on what might happen if sufficient effort were repeatedly applied in a new direction. Daydreaming is nothing more than the first stage of planning.

That's not to say every idea that emerges from my own daydreams turns out to be a good one. I estimate that perhaps one out of every ten ideas I come up with eventually materializes into a worthwhile project.

If I were a baseball player, I'd be batting a sorry .100, and I'd be sent back to the bush leagues. If I were a stockbroker, you'd promptly close your account. If I were a politician, my good-idea average would never produce enough votes to elect me to any office.

But philanthropy is different. Our profession lives or dies on the strength of creative new ideas—or at least it should.

Of course, most ideas will fail to mature from their zygote stage into the full-blown walking-around realm of programmatic success. But that's true with all creative endeavors. Many flawed ideas must be hatched, coddled, and finally sacrificed on the way to ideas that actually enjoy a reasonable chance of success. It takes time and perseverance, as well as imagination, to carve these possibilities from the granite of reality.

Ask Michelangelo.

In the end, the important thing is that you keep coming up with creative ideas.

Indeed, the encouragement and nurturing of the imagination should be one of the hallmarks of foundation life. And one of the truly wonderful benefits of empowering the imagination is that the effort proves self-replicating—sometimes even self-perpetuating. Imaginative people attract peers of a similar cast of mind. In fact, throughout history we've seen many instances of innovation and energy welling up in a single city or region so that eventually the name of the place itself becomes synonymous with creative achievement. Think fifteenth-century Florence, Philadelphia circa 1776, Silicon Valley today.

When I started my career in the 1960s, I was lucky to be situated in the San Francisco Bay Area. Back then, the region teemed with social experimentation, as countless people found themselves inflamed by the desire to *create* something new and better. To my mind, the decade exemplified the true meaning of the entrepreneurial spirit—which is very different from the oppositional spirit, our more conventional characterization of the sixties, with its need to confront, criticize, oppose, and prevent.

Why did so many creative minds gather in one place? Perhaps one reason—aside from the compelling fact that the Bay Area is a beautiful place to live—was our lack of a local aristocracy. In the post–World War II era, the West Coast still ranked as frontier territory, remote from the corridors of power in New York and Washington. This splendid isolation made the Bay Area a particularly democratic place, a meritocracy of newcomers. Wealth and tradition had yet to wall off the region's most creative thinkers. David Packard, cofounder of Hewlett-Packard as well as one of the country's most innovative foundations, was famous for his disinterest in all matters related to the *Social Register* and social pretensions. If you knocked on his door, he'd answer personally; if you had a good idea, he wanted to hear about it directly from you. This kind of attitude permeated our region, and it allowed ideas to percolate up from every stratum of society—to the benefit of all.

Another trait of a thriving culture of ideas is less obvious, perhaps even counterintuitive. People who trade in creativity usually refuse to take themselves too seriously. As I've emphasized throughout this book, failure is a key component of creativity, one of the stepping stones that lead eventually to success. A person burdened with too much self-seriousness would never be able to leap from stone to stone—from failure to failure to ultimate success. Creative people maintain a sense of humor about all things, including their own fallibility.

Where Do Ideas Come From?

WATCHING PEOPLE thrive in the entrepreneurial culture of the 1960s proved to me that much was possible, given the right dose of imagination and courage. Today I believe that in philanthropy, anything less than creative is insufficient.

But how do you keep the ideas flowing in the midst of so many other duties? Even within the trimmest, least paper-laden, most unbureaucratic foundation imaginable, there remains a myriad of tasks to juggle every day of the week.

I think the secret is rather simple.

You make creative thinking a personal and organizational priority.

It's crucial for me to spend some part of my workweek unoccupied by pressing duties and all-around busy-ness. I benefit from moments of utter silence, when I can actually hear my brain spinning its wheels. Ideas tumble through my mind in the shower, while mowing the lawn, as I plod along through insufferable traffic jams. I also take weekly piano lessons—which manage not only to free up my mind in entirely new ways as my fingers engage in ever more complicated contortions, but to reinforce my sense of humility through the daunting task of learning something new.

All that said, I'm not sure that it's possible to *will* new ideas into existence. But we certainly can create the conditions in which they emerge on their own. Most critically, we can step out from the cocoon of our own experience and stimulate our imaginations by meeting new people, engaging in debate about issues close to our hearts, and exploring organizations and parts of town that would otherwise remain unfamiliar.

Once again, I am making my case for one of philanthropy's first principles: get out of your office and thrust yourself into the larger world. The effort will inevitably lead to new perceptions, which will yield to new insights, which just may precipitate some worthwhile new ideas.

On a practical basis, you might benefit from the following:

- **Visit other foundations to see how they work.** Stay one or two full days, focus on good grants directed at important issues, rather than management procedures, and leave time to talk with staff. Ask lots of questions and take notes.

- **Get up from your desk and move around.** A day behind the computer screen is enough to put anybody to sleep. Get up, take a walk, oxygenate your brain, and reroute yourself from the grooves of familiar thinking.

- **Let creativity grow contagious.** Schedule idea-swapping sessions with your staff. Brainstorm issues with the help of a skilled facilitator. Drive deeply into your organization the conviction that imaginative ideas are valued.

- **Stay positive.** Encourage a positive frame of reference as opposed to a reactive stance. Set aside your own negative feelings or lack of confidence and try to move naysayers along in a similar fashion. Attitude is a matter of habit—and it's just as easy to cultivate good habits as bad.

- **Don't worry (yet) about the ramifications of an idea.** What if a million people apply, what if we run out of money, what if we can't make it work? These concerns can and must be dealt with eventually—but not in the brainstorming stage. Your unfettered imagination will almost certainly produce some ideas that prove loopy, impractical, too idealistic, or too ambitions. On the other hand, your impractical ideas might simply be ahead of their time, their virtues unrecognized because they've yet to be put into practice. Most ideas deserve a chance to live and breathe, and perhaps one day stand on their own two feet. Postpone judgments about what will work and what won't until you move beyond the brainstorming stage.

Ideas into Action

MOST FOUNDATIONS place the grantmaking cart before the horse.

The staff and board debate, decide upon, and then publish "funding priorities." When the proposals arrive, most are rejected out of hand because they do not fit the foundation's wish list of interests.

Yet within every batch of rejected proposals there probably reside a few gems—original, untested, and potentially transformative ideas whose greatest flaws, as far as the funders are concerned, lie in their originality.

While it's certainly standard grantmaking practice, it doesn't make sense to exclusively consider proposals that already fit your foundation's mold of acceptable ideas. We need to extend our reach beyond the doorstep of everyday expectations—while not straying too drastically from our areas of expertise.

Here are a few projects we funded at PVF that never would have made it through the first cut if we had eliminated the unexpected and irregular:

Scholarships for the trades: Donors love to give money to hardworking, motivated students who would otherwise not be able to attend college. But what about all the students who don't make A's—who aren't even destined for college? That's the question we kept asking ourselves, and eventually, we hit upon a means to reach young people in poor communities equipped with the potential to succeed, despite their modest academic achievements.

To begin, we focused on tools. We teamed up with the carpentry, auto shop, and metal work instructors at our local community colleges and asked them to identify particularly keen students who possessed everything they needed to succeed in their trades except the tools. We provided the lion's share of the tools' cost, but never the entire amount. For a car mechanic completing his training, the complete set of tools could run up to six thousand dollars. We'd ask the student to pay one-third, thereby reinforcing his sense of ownership and participation in determining his own future.

Our program turned the tables on academic scholarships. Instead of providing entrance money to help freshmen through their first uncertain year of college—a time when inadequately prepared students flunk out at high rates—we back-loaded the process, helping trade-school students who had already proved their mettle but still lacked the means to advance their careers. We often worked with young men and women in their mid and late twenties—people bypassed at a critical moment in their personal and professional development because of the tacit assumption that they had "already had their chance." Over the years, our scholarships in the trades have expanded to include people training to become cosmetologists and men and women of all ages requiring uniforms or union membership fees to secure a steady job. It's not how they handle scholarships at Harvard, Stanford, or Berkeley, but it works.

Day off programs for respite and inspiration: Our Day Off Program for poor women showed us that a very small amount of money could go a long way in bolstering an individual's self-worth—while also addressing, in admittedly a small way, the glaring inequities in our society. So we decided to extend our experiment by offering a similar opportunity to people serving as unpaid caregivers for disabled and chronically ill family members. By definition, these caregivers are invisible and neglected—and a day off means a great deal to them.

A variation on this theme also worked for teachers. We asked school principals to select talented novices who could benefit from a day spent observing a classroom veteran at another school. We paid for the substitute teacher, lunch money, mileage, and a fifty-dollar stipend to the host teacher.

Rent that makes sense: During the course of our work in a poor immigrant community, we learned that families routinely paid thirteen hundred dollars monthly to live in unconverted garages. The accommodations proved both miserable and expensive, but without access to credit or a large amount of cash, even people with steady jobs found they couldn't rent apartments. We worked with an immigrant rights organization to establish a no-interest loan fund to cover the families' first and last months' rent and utility deposits. With this small bit of assistance, a family could move into a two-bedroom apartment for the same amount they had been paying for substandard, unsanitary accommodations.

An unexpected outcome of the arts: Think for a moment about teen pregnancy, a "problem" that persists despite decades of incentive programs and counseling. We knew that we didn't have "the solution," but when we were approached by Ehud Krauss, director of the Zohar Dance Company in Palo Alto, we thought we had better listen to what he'd discovered. Ehud explained that one of the benefits of drawing low-income girls into his rigorous program of modern dance training turned out to be a complete absence of teenage pregnancies among the participants. That certainly wasn't

Ehud's initial goal, but he recognized the effect. So we backed his work, not as arts funding, but in an effort to stem the number of teen pregnancies in the neighborhood. Soon he was working with several after-school groups, as well as a project at Juvenile Hall—and having a huge impact on kids who would otherwise not experience the training, discipline, and personal satisfactions of becoming dancers.

Talking Ideas into Existence

SOMETIMES IDEAS arrive in a moment of inspiration from one of our staff. More often, they emerge over weeks, months, or even years, as a part of our continuing conversation with outstanding people in the community.

I recall talking with a sheriff in Half Moon Bay, a small coastal town south of San Francisco, and learning that interactions between law enforcement and teenage drivers had been taking a decidedly negative turn. So the sheriff and I started brainstorming. How, we wondered, might the meeting of cops, kids, and cars be a good experience for everybody? We decided to sponsor a car rally along with the Highway Patrol and the local police department. We gave trophies for the most stylish small car, big car, paint job, and detailing. We ran a "safe driving slalom" in which the kids had to run the course at a precise speed—neither too fast nor too slow. The event cost our foundation $250, proved a huge success, established personal contacts between local teenagers and law enforcement, and made the community feel safer.

And it all happened because the sheriff and I took the time to talk together.

Another time, I set up interviews with low-income high school students in West Oakland so I could learn from them directly what it's like to be sixteen years old in their neighborhood—the difficulties and the opportunities facing them. We spoke about their work aims. One wanted to become a real estate agent and another an architect. So a few days later, I contacted some local businesspeople in those fields to see if they'd take on an intern for the summer. Our foundation paid a stipend to the kids and they spent the summer learning just what the working world is really like.

So where *do* ideas come from?

It's my conviction that it's the combination of repose and conversation—a commitment to quiet time spent pondering what might be achieved, coupled with vigorous, ongoing relationships with the community's outstanding agencies and individuals. Creative thinking is what gets sparked between these two poles—the electricity that illuminates our grantmaking and keeps us all feeling inspired and alive.

8 Philanthropy as Action

Principle #5:

Take initiative

> *"You must be the change you wish to see in the world."*
>
> *—Mahatma Gandhi*

"MONEY IS LIKE MANURE," wrote Thornton Wilder, the great American playwright and author of *Our Town*. "It's not worth a thing unless it's spread around encouraging young things to grow."

Wilder certainly pegged the potential of money to do good. But I prefer another metaphor.

I like to think of money as energy. Like an electric current, money must be put into circulation to achieve its ultimate purpose. Once circulating, it then becomes a powerful force—driving action, illuminating events, enlivening institutions.

In short, money justifies its own existence only when it's plugged into worthwhile endeavors. Otherwise, it just sits there, and as Wilder implies, begins to smell—an untapped resource going to waste.

Let me explain.

Not long ago, I had lunch with the managing director of a large professional sports organization. I made the appointment because I had heard a story around town about one of his team's rookies. This young man, only a year or so out of college, had misplaced his wallet one day following a workout. In addition to the usual hassle of replacing his credit cards, driver's license, and other personal items, the player was miffed because some cash had also disappeared.

In his wallet, he'd been carrying five thousand dollars.

When anybody misplaces five thousand dollars of walking-around money, you know that something more important has also been lost. I thought about all the young athletes in our country who make three, five, ten million dollars a year. How many of them contemplate the possibility of becoming true "sports heroes" by giving back even a modest portion of their incomes in the form of philanthropy?

Very few—and the main reason for this is that nobody shows them how.

So I sat down with the team's managing director, and I offered to coach his players on how to give effectively, pointing out that a good grantmaker needs some of the same qualities a good ball-player has: energy, strategy, and initiative. He liked the idea. It's something we're going to build on in the future.

I know that the team's managing director also liked the fact that in contacting him I had shown initiative of my own.

Americans value initiative very highly—far more than most societies. We idealize the pioneer, the entrepreneur, the self-made man and woman.

Initiative should also be prized in grantmaking.

Indeed, it ranks as the final component required to achieve philanthropic excellence. And it's the only quality that will enable us to reach out and tap the unrealized potential of a great swath of American society—from professional athletes walking around with too much money in their pockets to the millionaire next door.

Initiative and Philanthropic Ventures Foundation

AS I HAVE repeatedly emphasized, we place a premium at Philan-thropic Ventures Foundation (PVF) on getting out of the office and into the community to work with outstanding individuals in local voluntary organizations. We *expect* our staff to exercise initiative on a daily basis. But initiative means a good deal more than locat-ing nonprofit leaders and then coordinating efforts with them. We must also be prepared to take a critical second look at problems that once appeared intractable—and be willing to try something new.

Here are a few examples where initiative in our grantmaking at PVF paid off:

We know that two-thirds of teenage mothers with one child at home will have a second child within two years. As a result, these young, one-parent families will be mired in poverty with no road out. How can girls be persuaded not to bring another child into the world until they are emotionally and financially prepared? At PVF, we invested a small amount of grant money to delve into the core of this dilemma. Over one year, we funded a local com-munity organization to gather groups of ten teenage mothers at neighbors' homes with a trained adult facilitator. The facilitator's mission: lead the girls in frank discussions of the difficulties they now faced daily as new mothers. The discussions broke through the isolation most experienced, the project cost little—and two years later, none of the participants had a second child.

For four years, PVF supported a public high school located near our office in one of Oakland's poorest neighborhoods. Most of our grants aimed to advance literacy and math skills, while boosting the motivation of students already lagging far behind in state standard-ized testing. But over the years, we also noticed that many students had to cope with a range of serious health problems—untreated infections, asthma, injuries from street violence and parental abuse, dental pain, sexually transmitted diseases, and severe depression and anxiety. So we added another plank to our grantmaking platform and joined forces with Oakland's Children's Hospital, the County of Alameda, FACES of the Future, the UC Berkeley School of Optometry, and the Alameda County Dental Association to build a fully staffed health clinic on campus—with substantial support contributed by the San Francisco Foundation and the Hewlett Foundation. None of us would have tackled the project alone. But together, energized by a small jolt of foundation funding at the outset from PVF, we managed to start a high school health clinic that reached the teens most in need in our neighborhood.

Homelessness has long been an issue of concern at PVF, and we've supported a number of effective agencies and individuals working to get people off the streets. Despite the enormity and complexity of this problem, I know that we've made an important contribution. Yet after a while, I also came to realize that although I knew something about the issue of "homelessness," my acquaintance with homeless *people* had been limited over the years to a handful of brief conversations. I needed to understand the issue intellectually, emotionally, psychologically, experientially. So I asked the director of one homeless agency if I could spend a night on the street assisting his staff. We began the evening shift at the agency's modest offices, sorting through drawers of "street essentials": clothes, condoms, toiletries, candy bars, bandages, blankets—and most important, clean dry socks. Over the course of the night, I began to understand the problems faced by people living on the streets in a way I could not have grasped by reading about it or even talking with the most experienced professionals. Today when I think about homeless people, I find that I'm incapable of reducing their plight to an abstraction or a set of statistics. Rather, I remember faces, names, and personal histories of the people I met on the street that night. My time on the night shift proved an important step in my own education, as well as PVF's grantmaking strategies for reducing homelessness. But it never would have happened if I hadn't asked the director to make a place for me alongside his staff. The director later told me that no other funder had ever made a similar request. I wish I could say that surprised me, but I know that most grantmakers do not picture themselves working into the wee hours in their community's poorest neighborhoods and most dangerous streets. Yet I think that's exactly where we belong—at least a few times in our careers. If we're to acquire the knowledge and understanding that philanthropy requires, and then effectively help the people most in need, we must journey outside our own comfort zones.

Institutionalizing Initiative at Home and Abroad

WHEN IT COMES to effective grantmaking, individual initiative isn't enough. It's our duty as foundation directors and trustees to transform initiative into an institutional value. And how might this be accomplished? For me, one of the best examples is embodied in the remarkable work of Generosity in Action, founded by Duncan Beardsley.

While heading up the alumni travel and study program at Stanford University, Duncan recognized that affluent visitors to the Third World often returned home feeling their journeys were still somehow incomplete. They spoke warmly about the hospitality they encountered among people in Asia, Africa, Latin America, and the Middle East—but they also expressed concern about the profound needs they witnessed in terms of public health, education, and economic development. They wanted to help, but how? Rendering on-the-spot assistance almost never made sense. One-time visitors lacked the means of judging the wisdom and utility of a project, as well as the ability to organize, oversee, and gather together sufficient funds to pay for any substantive improvements.

In other words, the individual's impulse to do good required an organizational structure.

That's why Duncan founded Generosity in Action, and then joined forces with PVF. By working together, we've helped travelers dispense school supplies to a small village in the Amazon; dig clean water wells in a number of villages in Burma; build schools in Zambia and Niger; equip a nursery school in South Africa; and supply sewing machines and fabric to a women's cooperative near Mount Kilimanjaro. Each effort represents a perfect marriage between personal initiative and collective follow-through. The traveler identifies a need, confirms its significance with the local people, raises money among friends and colleagues back in the U.S.—and then arranges the operational details to make certain that everything unfolds as planned. PVF provides the tax-exempt status to handle donations. We allocate money as needed to a supervisor on site. And then we coordinate continuous oversight with tour operators and educational travel programs, who return to the project and track progress over time. In a program characterized by immense distance between donors and doers, we all work as a team to ensure an extremely high degree of accountability. Indeed, during the course of a project to put a well in a Zambian village, we received photos and reports on four separate occasions: the day that workers dug the hole, the week a construction crew built the well, the moment villagers drew the first bucket of clean water, and months later, when it had become a daily routine for families to line up for drinking and washing water.

Research and Wasted Effort: Do You Need a Needs Assessment?

MANY GRANTMAKERS succumb to the occupational hazard of studying problems into the ground.

Recognizing an obvious need in their community—say, the shortage of affordable housing or low academic achievement among immigrant children—they'll commission an expansive paper, report, or even a book that will rain down upon the issue a blizzard of statistics, anecdotes, and sociological analysis.

Too often, these commissioned studies substitute for action. The papers, reports, and books get filed away, usually unread, and the problem persists. Nobody has a stake in translating theory into practice.

Equally time-consuming, costly, and unproductive can be the formal "needs assessment" of local conditions.

It's understandable why new funders—particularly fledgling community foundations—might believe they require a needs assessment. Their staff and trustees want to know what's happening in their community, where the direst problems reside, how they might begin to remedy them. Yet is it really necessary to commission a study to know that your city is facing a crisis in public education and homelessness? That your rural community is beset by a shortage of doctors and limited career options for young people? That your state is confronting the AIDS pandemic, youth violence, a shrinking blue collar job base, and the lack of universal health care coverage?

We don't need another fifty-page report outlining the local contours of our nation's famously abiding crises—particularly if the report argues the self-evident, postpones action, and takes so long to complete that the situation has already changed before the ink is dry.

The most useful needs assessment comes from getting out into your community, meeting people, asking a million questions, observing everything. The philanthropist should be his own best social scientist, reporter, and sleuth.

Am I taking an anti-intellectual stance here, arguing against study, information, and facts? Not at all. What I'm suggesting is that in most cases, we do not "need more study of policy" because those studies are already sitting on the shelves of any number of excellent public policy study groups operating out of New York, Texas, California, Michigan, Illinois, and elsewhere. We can benefit from reading their work and talking to their staffs; not by attempting to recycle or reinvent their efforts.

In terms of background and context, you can profitably begin with a trip to your local public library. An excellent journalistic account of drug addiction, homelessness, or the crisis in public education—or better yet, *three* excellent accounts, from contrasting points of view—will do more to educate you and cost far less than any study you might commission. The authors of the best nonfiction work spend several years investigating their subjects, frequently dispelling the conventional wisdom with accurate on-the-ground reporting. This kind of investigation requires total immersion in the subject and, as a result, provides far more information and context than any study could hope to relay. Plus, these works frequently enjoy the virtue of being engrossing good reads.

Taking the Initiative by Convening

WHAT'S THE ALTERNATIVE when you want to learn more about an issue and then explore a range of possible strategies to improve community life?

I remain a staunch advocate of convening.

Convening is the art of bringing together the *real* experts, the local nonprofit people who grapple with issues and actions on a daily basis. Once gathered in a small group, these folks can:

- Generate insights drawn from their extensive experience
- Form partnerships
- Craft objectives, strategies, and activities
- Guide your own funding priorities

What constitutes a convening?

When you bring together a half-dozen organizations in your community working to stem teenage drug use through a variety of strategies—and then ask them to inform you and one another about what works for each of them and what doesn't—this gathering can be fairly termed a convening.

On the other hand, if you summon the same agencies to announce to them what *you* have concluded regarding how *they* should approach drug abuse—even going so far as to unveil a roster of new funding priorities (which you've devised entirely on your own)—then you are not promoting the dialogue, learning, and mutual benefits that characterize a genuine convening.

Let me give you an example of what I mean by convening from our experience at PVF.

Over the years, PVF has maintained an interest in promoting literacy. We see adult literacy as the necessary prerequisite to advancing job opportunities and achieving economic self-sufficiency. Among young people, literacy stands as the gateway to all other academic pursuits. What's more, it can be a tool in nourishing the imagination, expanding a sense of possibility, and quelling youth violence. After all, the young person equipped with the ability to read has the entire world open to him, while the illiterate is consigned to the gritty here, now, and forever of mean streets and dead ends.

In short, we knew that we wanted to throw extra support behind literacy efforts, particularly among youth. But we didn't know what steps to take next. So we gathered together the people in our region who make literacy their profession—the head librarians of our region's small towns, suburbs, and cities.

Of course, many of these folks already knew one another from conferences and professional meetings. But they had never met before under the auspices of a third party to frankly discuss the problems impeding their progress—and then take action to remedy them. We explained to the librarians that we wanted to learn from their experience and then see if there was some small way that we could help them.

Over the course of a long day's meeting, we heard the discussion emphasize two main points:

- Libraries were having trouble expanding their base among young people, immigrants, and the poor.

- Librarians remained confident that they could make progress with a small amount of financial support and the leeway to craft programs to suit their particular communities.

So PVF launched its Library Resource Grants Program, supplying main and branch librarians with small grants to experiment and see what worked to attract new patrons. Later, we all agreed, we would get back together and share information about what succeeded and what fell short.

Over the course of the year, we made ninety-eight grants totaling $44,912 at sixty-nine public libraries. Our average grant was small: $458. But the librarians proved remarkably creative in reaching teens, early readers, emergent English learners, and people who typically do not use libraries.

In Daly City, the librarian attracted teens to the summer reading program by hiring a local artist to lead a cartooning workshop. In Santa Clara, the library partnered with Kaiser Hospital to place picture books in the hands of young children during pediatric clinic visits. Library volunteers then read aloud to the children, and pediatricians talked with parents about the importance of reading at home to their young children. In Mountain View, the librarian brought in Spanish-speaking performing artists—resulting in an unprecedented surge in new requests for library cards and spiking the circulation rates for Spanish-language books and magazines. Other projects included teen poetry contests, children's story hours, phonics workshops, puppets promoting reading, book bags and books that children could take home, reading clubs, tutoring programs, and appearances by children's authors.

Of course, I'm pointing to an example of convening that concluded precisely as planned, with all parties reaping benefits. It doesn't always turn out that way. I also know from experience that convening can prove a complicated affair even for a seasoned grantmaker. Most difficult to negotiate is the imbalance of power. Simply put, you hold most of the cards when it comes to convening. When you invite participants, they *will* come—if only because of their hope that you might one day fund their organization. But given that you're unlikely to make grants to everybody at the table—indeed, you may end up supporting none of them—the potential for resentment and mistrust looms large. Over the years, I've found that the following considerations improve the chances of success:

1. **Clear purpose:** Be honest about the reasons for initiating the convening—with the participants and yourself. If your aim is simply to learn more about a topic, make that clear. If you hope for a more ambitious—if yet undefined—outcome, then be equally frank. Make your invitations personally to each participant. Let each individual know who else is invited. Stress your desire to learn from the gathering, and live up to your promise.

2. **Flexibility:** Count on the unexpected to happen, and be ready to bend with the weight of its implications. After all, that's the entire point of the gathering: to catch a glimpse of what's happening beneath the surface of events, and shift your own grantmaking efforts accordingly (while still holding true to the essence of your inquiry). If you already knew what would happen and what would be said, there would be no need to hold the convening.

3. **Openness:** Learning to listen with open minds and open hearts is a challenge for all philanthropists. We get in a habit of expecting others to attend to our viewpoint—which they usually do, since we hold the purse strings. But if you aren't prepared to pay attention to information and opinions that may surprise, dismay, and even displease you—along with all the good stuff—then stay away from convening.

4. **Frankness about future funding:** Every nonprofit at your convening will be speculating about the grant you could

make to them one bright future day. It's human nature; it's also what we expect from motivated leaders. Don't fight it, and don't ignore it. Instead, handle the funding issue explicitly. Do not dangle the prospect of extensive support when you have not yet made a firm decision or consulted with your board.

Getting the Word Out

ALL BUT THE largest foundations tend to neglect a crucial aspect of their mission—the publicizing of their funding interests, and the propagation of their achievements within the larger community.

Why should grantmakers care about public relations? By discussing your work in the media, you can:

- Inform the community at large about your foundation's goals and activities
- Alert the organizations and individuals you want to support
- Add to the public's understanding of philanthropy
- Attract additional donors

In truth, foundation activities can turn out to be an easy sell to the media. That's something we discovered at PVF in 2001, when we negotiated an arrangement with a local television news affiliate which gave us four minutes of early morning air time to discuss our current round of funding initiatives. I went on air the first time to alert science and art teachers to our new fax grants. When I got back to the office, our phone had already begun to ring with enthusiastic inquiries. Not from teachers; they hadn't seen the broadcast, since they were already at work. But many parents watched, and they immediately picked up the phone to pepper us with questions about how their children's favorite teachers could apply. That first day, we received more than four hundred calls, with our fax machine churning incessantly. Over the next week, four hundred more inquiries came our way—including many from teachers acting on tips from interested parents.

Before this announcement, I'd never considered the potential of broadcast media. But it turned out to be a tremendous boon. Over the year, I returned to the station a half-dozen times to talk for several minutes each broadcast about seventeen different program areas we were then funding. Over one million Bay Area residents watched these broadcasts. Even today, I run into people on the street who tell me, "I know you. You're that guy on TV who gives away money to good causes. Now tell me more about what all you do…"

I learned something important from this experience. I'd always known that our grantmaking was important, but it also turned out that to be *newsworthy*—something that I'd never thought about before. And if *our* grantmaking is newsworthy, within the highly competitive media market of the San Francisco Bay Area, the same holds true for foundations located elsewhere. Newspapers, radio, and current events shows on television in all parts of the country never quite get their fill; they are hungry maws always needing to be fed information. Foundations should dedicate themselves to nourishing their local media with tasty morsels about their funding goals and achievements. Of course, it's not always an easy sell—and you certainly shouldn't expect the media to find you. Like most of American society, journalists tend to be uninformed about philanthropy. But the potential benefits of getting the word out about your grantmaking via broadcast and print media remain enormous.

Community Foundations: Initiative Where It's Needed Most

OVER THE YEARS, I've visited and counseled more than three hundred community foundations throughout the country. Most of them were established over the past two decades—they were the growth sector of contemporary philanthropy.

And I've found that when faced with the prospect of opening a new community foundation, most directors and trustees ask three questions:

- What are the rules?
- What is my role?
- How do other foundations behave?

Reasonable queries, to be sure. It's only natural that novice grantmakers should want to slip into the mainstream of the foundation world and begin their enterprise by retracing the steps of more experienced peers. The problem, as I see it, is that while more established foundations may exhibit reasonable standards of fairness and sound management, their grantmaking—the very reason for their existence—remains lackluster and unimaginative. Trailing after their example only leads back to more of the same: insular factory philanthropy.

A far better question—or at least, the question that should be asked upon setting up a community foundation, and then returned to persistently over the years—is this:

What do we want to achieve, and how can we get it done?

Asking this fundamental two-part question about aims and means will inevitably throw newcomers into conflict with many philanthropic conventions: the reliance on applications, the bureaucratic roundabout of proposal review, the isolation of foundation staff and trustees.

From my perspective, that's all to the good.

Community foundations should serve as the free agents of initiative philanthropy. Liberated from the whims of misguided or uninformed relatives who dominate many family foundations, or the economic and political imperatives of corporate philanthropy, community foundations stand ideally suited to explore, experiment, and forge alliances with disparate organizations and motivated individuals. *They don't have to do what everybody else is doing.* Indeed, given their parochial nature—their charter to address local needs exclusively—they should *not* be replicating the strategies of their peers.

Let me explain how I think community foundations (and most private foundations) could vastly improve their performance by taking more initiative.

- **Reframe the terms of success.** Many community foundations measure progress by the size of their endowments and the growth of their investments. Of course, it's necessary to keep an eye on the bottom line, but that's hardly the sum of success. The real goal is effective philanthropy: imaginative, enterprising grantmaking linked to outstanding organizations and individuals.

- **Conduct your own research.** I've seen many new community foundations launch their grantmaking programs by commissioning a five-thousand-dollar formal needs analysis conducted by a professional researcher, academic, or consultant. Not only does this action postpone meeting local needs; it constitutes a breach of fundamental duties. The community foundation's staff should take as their first responsibility the exploration of local needs, players, and potential. This kind of learning cannot be deputized.

- **Seek the obvious ally.** In the San Francisco Bay Area, where I live, we stand waist deep in nonprofit organizations of every stripe and variety. But that's not true for Trinity County, some three hundred miles to our north—or for most of the rural townships and small cities in each of the fifty states that have recently established community foundations. Outside the metropolitan hubs, the dominant players in education, the arts, and social welfare tend to be government agencies supported (however uncertainly) by tax revenues. Yet most foundations shy away from collaborating with public agencies, as though the nonprofit and public sectors somehow constitute incompatible realms. In truth, government agencies often provide direct access to many communities' most motivated change makers.

- **Make applications easy.** Long, complicated application forms replicate the worst of government and foundation funding. Your forms should be brief. They also should prove useful, rather than onerous, to applicants. Good applications ask questions which applicants find value in trying to answer. And how might you know what questions those are? Ask the applicants themselves. It's a good place to start a lifetime of frank conversation.

- **Think local.** For years, foundations have nursed along the falsehood that you can ship ideas around the country and get the same results everywhere. In truth, what works swimmingly in one place belly flops in another. Why aren't more ideas transportable? Because the critical aspect of every project is the quality of its leadership. Community foundations should base their work less on the shining successes of other communities than on people in their midst.

The Limits of Personal and Organizational Initiative

FOR ALL ITS VIRTUES, initiative grantmaking also has its limitations.

Most obviously, it won't work with weak collaborators. If you're a funder bursting with ideas, energy, and the willingness to take risks, you need alliances with people in the nonprofit sector who are strong and knowledgeable. Ideal collaborators possess sufficient confidence to reject your bad ideas, and enough experience and insight to perceive a glimmer of good in an otherwise flawed concept—and then persevere alongside you to craft a better alternative.

Initiative grantmaking is also tempered by matters of size and scale. At PVF, we fund projects throughout the San Francisco Bay Area, the nation's fourth largest metropolitan region. We focus on locating outstanding leaders and giving them free creative rein in discrete pockets of the community that they know best. It's an approach that gets significant but measured results. It doesn't transform the world utterly or overnight.

We don't tackle projects beyond the scope of our modest resources. Despite the temptations, we will never attempt to untangle the Bay Area's nightmare commute by underwriting massive public transportation projects or launch bottom-up reforms to transform our national health care system. Traffic and universal health care, along with comprehensive economic development, school reform, and so many other righteous aims, require large-scale private and public investment. And though we frequently work with folks who have fenced off a small corner of these big problems to render some immediate assistance to a limited number of people, we do not suffer from delusions of grandeur regarding our ability to burrow into vast and intricate public policy issues and emerge with *the* answer.

Does that mean grantmakers of limited size must content themselves with treating their communities' ills with figurative Band-Aids?

Not at all. We know our limits—but only because we've repeatedly tested them. At PVF, we strive for systemic changes in our society. Along the way, we also try to aid the individuals who have nowhere else to turn. We recognize that our society's needs are deep and multifarious, and we must work everywhere at once. We also admit to ourselves that we will not achieve all of our goals during our collective lifetimes, never mind within the course of a single career.

But instead of dwelling on what lies beyond reach, I often find myself reflecting upon the prospect of social tipping points—the means by which small improvements on a continuing basis trigger widespread change. I'm thinking of communities that have decreased homicide rates through incremental advances in police response rates, or graffiti eradication programs that transform blighted neighborhoods by attracting new businesses, foot traffic, and increased residential density. I believe that if we all keep working with the smartest, most dedicated people in our midst, then we'll make progress. At any moment, the odds are stacked against us as grantmakers, but time is on our side.

Beyond Initiative: Generosity and Sacrifice

GENEROSITY is a virtue that rewards the giver at least as much as the recipient. The Bible tells us, "A generous man will himself be blessed." A Buddhist teaching asks, "Have you ever met a generous, unhappy person?"

Truly, it is better to give than to receive. That's something grasped by all adults—and I'm speaking here in terms of psychological, ethical, and spiritual development, not merely years. Yet sometimes I wonder if philanthropy couldn't boost its impact and effectiveness by embracing another traditional virtue.

I think we have to seriously consider the prospect of sacrifice.

Sacrifice is a word seldom spoken in the foundation world. What does it mean in the context of grantmaking?

A foundation embracing a modest aspect of sacrifice might move beyond the annual pay-out provision of 5 percent in its grantmaking to 10 or even 15 percent—and scarcely notice the difference. Philanthropists with an appetite for larger sacrifices might dip into their principal. A few foundations have wholly sacrificed their very existence, strategically planning their own obsolescence as they spend down assets over a fixed period and finally close their doors for good.

To my eyes, the justification of philanthropic sacrifice lies in the needs that surround us—the pain, suffering, and injustice that can be denied only by those who shut their eyes against it.

"In the world as it is now," asserts the philosopher Peter Singer, "I can see no escape from the conclusion that each one of us with wealth surplus to his or her essential needs should be giving most of it to help people suffering from poverty so dire as to be life-threatening. That's right: I'm saying that you shouldn't buy that new car, take that cruise, redecorate the house, or get that pricey new suit. After all, a $1,000 suit could save five children's lives."

And what might Singer say about a foundation that devotes its limited assets to redecorating its new offices or padding an executive compensation package to approximate the perks of a corporate CEO? "Again," he reminds us, "the formula is simple: whatever money you're spending on luxuries, not necessities, should be given away."

That's a stiff standard, one that few of us are willing to embrace. But its severity also puts philanthropy in perspective. Aren't we obliged to make greater efforts to ameliorate the lot of people suffering in our midst? Not just as individuals, but in our professional roles—as grantmakers, with our millions and billions of dollars growing fatter each year inside our coffers?

Sacrifice in grantmaking means getting along with less: less money accumulating in our portfolios, less status, power, and self-regard in our professional roles. Most of all—and most satisfying to achieve—it means less bureaucracy, routine, and paper pushing dedicated to monotonous, expensive, and unproductive labors. As grantmakers, we must be willing to shed the protective coating of philanthropic formality, flee our desks, and enter the unpredictable realms of the underprivileged in order to change the world.

Seven Immodest Proposals

To Make Philanthropy More Effective,
Exciting, and Fun

1. **Get out of the office and into the field at least 30 percent of the time.** Almost everything you need to know as a grantmaker is taking place beyond your office doors. Devote as much time as possible to exploring unfamiliar corners of your community to learn what's happening on the ground. Get out of your comfort zone. Meet people undertaking important, creative projects and start building productive, long-term relationships. Begin now by making a commitment to spend at least 30 percent of your time in the field—and over time allow that commitment to grow.

2. **Pare back the paper to a slim stack.** Foundation philanthropy is drowning in paper. Start bailing out your own office by working towards paperless giving. Spend less

time on proposals that will inevitably be denied. Ask
your applicants for the bare minimum of documentation
required for you to make informed decisions. Eliminate
duplicate copies. Pick up the telephone when potential
grantees call, and stem the flow of proposals unrelated
to your interests and needs.

3. **Speed up your response time.** Nonprofits shouldn't have
   to wait months for an answer to their funding requests—
   and grantmakers shouldn't waste their own time with protracted and redundant deliberations. Set up systems that
   allow your staff to respond rapidly to proposals. Be willing to trust more. Experiment with immediate response
   grants made by the foundation staff and dispatch checks
   in less than a week. Avoid all but the most crucial meetings. Forge a reputation for swift decision making and
   enshrine speed and simplicity as the organizational
   watchwords.

4. **Empower the executive to make grants without board
   approval.** If your board has clearly articulated its mission, the executive shouldn't need to consult its members to approve every grant. Authorize the executive
   to make grants—be they five thousand dollars or fifty
   thousand dollars. You'll save time, reduce bureaucracy,
   clarify management and governance functions, and build
   trust throughout the foundation. Most important, you
   will reposition your foundation to aid nonprofits at the
   moment of maximum impact.

5. **Establish a venture fund for riskier grants.** It's easier to take
   risks on promising, but unproven, ventures if you're prepared both fiscally and psychologically. Set up a venture
   philanthropy fund, designating a sum for use exclusively
   on high-risk, high-impact projects. A commitment to

risk-taking within prescribed limits will energize grant-making, encourage initiative and innovation, and attract more imaginative projects from applicants.

6. **Fund outstanding individuals engaged in important work.** Most foundations limit their grantmaking to 501(c)(3) organizations, confusing tax-exempt status with the legal requirements for "charitable giving." This policy sacrifices potential partnerships with highly motivated, entrepreneurial individuals working outside the conventional nonprofit structure. Revisit your policy regarding support for individuals and experiment with grants to outstanding people who you meet through your continuing exploration of the community.

7. **Link large foundations with smaller community foundations to pursue grassroots grantmaking.** Many large foundations that deal in national or global issues cannot devote staff or resources to the relatively smaller goals of local grantmaking. But they can delegate—by supporting well-run community foundations whose staffs make a special effort to get out of their offices and identify the people strategically suited to make a difference locally. Initiate partnerships between your region's largest funders and its community foundations, and work together to make certain that grassroots philanthropy gets an opportunity to flourish.

And finally...Make sure your work remains exciting, inspired, and fun. Grantmaking should be a joyous vocation. After all, you're dealing with interesting people, important issues, and the very real possibility of improving the world. In short, you're perfectly positioned for a satisfying life—one enriched by social contacts, commitments, and contributions to the commonweal.

HEYDAY INSTITUTE

Since its founding in 1974, Heyday Books has occupied a unique niche in the publishing world, specializing in books that foster an understanding of the history, literature, art, environment, social issues, and culture of California and the West. We are a 501(c)(3) nonprofit organization based in Berkeley, California, serving a wide range of people and audiences.

We are grateful for the generous funding we've received for our publications and programs during the past year from foundations and more than three hundred individual donors. Major supporters include:

Anonymous; Anthony Andreas, Jr.; Barnes & Noble bookstores; BayTree Fund; B.C.W. Trust III; S. D. Bechtel, Jr. Foundation; Fred & Jean Berensmeier; Book Club of California; Butler Koshland Fund; California Council for the Humanities; California State Library; Candelaria Fund; Columbia Foundation; Compton Foundation, Inc.; Federated Indians of Graton Rancheria; Fleishhacker Foundation; Wallace Alexander Gerbode Foundation; Marion E. Greene; Walter & Elise Haas Fund; Leanne Hinton; Hopland Band of Pomo Indians; James Irvine Foundation; George Frederick Jewett Foundation; Marty Krasney; Guy Lampard & Suzanne Badenhoop; LEF Foundation; Robert Levitt; Michael McCone; Middletown Rancheria Tribal Council; National Audubon Society; National Endowment for the Arts; National Park Service; Philanthropic Ventures Foundation; Poets & Writers; Rim of the World Interpretive Association; River Rock Casino; Riverside-Corona Resource Conservation; Alan Rosenus; San Francisco Foundation; Santa Ana Watershed Association; William Saroyan Foundation; Seaver Institute; Sandy Cold Shapero; Service Plus Credit Union; L. J. Skaggs and Mary C. Skaggs Foundation; Skirball Foundation; Swinerton Family Fund; Thendara Foundation; Victorian Alliance; Tom White; Harold & Alma White Memorial Fund; and Stan Yogi.

Heyday Institute Board of Directors

Michael McCone (chair), Barbara Boucke, Peter Dunckel, Karyn Flynn, Theresa Harlan, Leanne Hinton, Nancy Hom, Susan Ives, Marty Krasney, Guy Lampard, Lee Swenson, Jim Swinerton, Lynne Withey, Stan Yogi.

For more information about Heyday Institute, our publications and programs, please visit our website at www.heydaybooks.com.

About the Authors

Bill Somerville is a nationally recognized expert on creative grantmaking. He has consulted at over 350 community foundations in the United States, Canada, and the U.K. on innovative grantmaking and effective operations. He has over forty-seven years of experience with nonprofits, including seventeen years as executive director of the Peninsula Community Foundation, and he has taught courses on philanthropy at Stanford University and community colleges.

In 1991 he founded Philanthropic Ventures Foundation, which specializes in innovative, responsive approaches to grantmaking, such as "paperless" discretionary grants and grants with a 48-hour turnaround.

A recipient of the 2004 Gerbode Fellowship Award in recognition of outstanding achievement as a nonprofit executive, Bill is also a founding member of the Haas Center for Public Service's national advisory board, at Stanford University, and a member of the School of Social Welfare's advisory board, at the University of California, Berkeley.

Bill has lived in the same house for seventy-five years, which he shares with Joanne, his beloved wife of fifty years, their feisty dachshund, Axel, and four free-range hens that lay golden eggs.

Fred Setterberg is the coauthor of several books about the nonprofit sector and philanthropy, including *Grantmaking Basics*, with Colburn Wilbur and Barbara Kibbe, and *Beyond Profit*, with Kary Schulman.